CAMBRIDGE TRAVEL BOOKS

T0364286

THE
DISCOVERY OF AMERICA
1492–1584

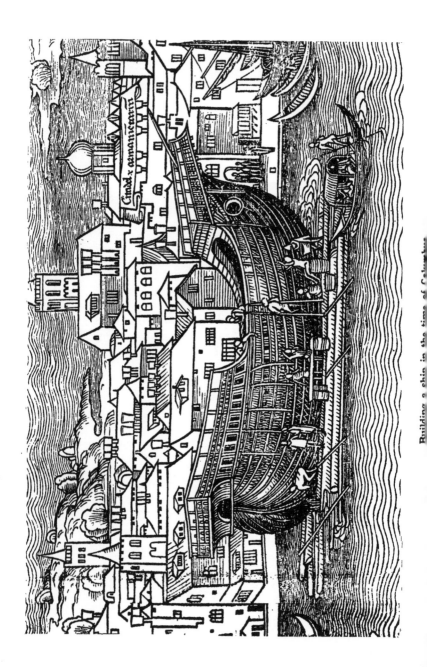

Building a ship in the time of Columbus

THE
DISCOVERY OF AMERICA
1492–1584

EDITED BY

PHILIP F. ALEXANDER, M.A.

HERTFORD COLLEGE, OXFORD

Cambridge :

at the University Press

1917

CAMBRIDGE UNIVERSITY PRESS
Cambridge, New York, Melbourne, Madrid, Cape Town,
Singapore, São Paulo, Delhi, Tokyo, Mexico City

Cambridge University Press
The Edinburgh Building, Cambridge CB2 8RU, UK

Published in the United States of America by
Cambridge University Press, New York

www.cambridge.org
Information on this title: www.cambridge.org/9781107600607

First published 1917
First paperback edition 2011

A catalogue record for this publication is available from the British Library

ISBN 978-1-107-60060-7 Paperback

PREFACE

THE aim of the present series is to illustrate the history of geographical discovery by means of select voyages and travels. These are usually written by the discoverer himself, or by an eye-witness who accompanied him on his journey. Apart from the results achieved, they are full of interest, since they tell the story of man's bravery in feeling his way over an unknown world.

The English voyages of the sixteenth century (some of which will be given in this series) record, moreover, the deeds of the seamen who laid the foundation of Britain's sea-power and of her Colonial Empire.

It is hoped that these books may be of service in schools, used either as Readers, or as an aid to the teaching of Geography. Spelling and punctuation have been modernized wherever necessary, though archaic words have been kept.

P. F. A.

WALBERSWICK,
May 1915.

The voyages chosen to illustrate the discovery of America can only cover a small part of so large a subject. Those of Columbus are the most important in this connection, as they are in the whole history of exploration. He was the first seaman who had the courage to sail far out of sight of land, and his example not only led to the knowledge of a New World, and all the quickening this knowledge produced in the mind of man, but also pointed the way to discovery in other directions.

Of the remaining voyages, that of the Frenchman, Jacques Cartier, is given both for its actual results and because it led afterwards to the French colonization of Canada. Sir Humfrey Gilbert is one of the forerunners of English colonization, and his voyage of 1583, though externally a failure, has a notable place in the history of the expansion of Britain. The expedition of Amadas and Barlow was sent out by Sir Walter Ralegh, and took possession by his directions of the piece of land, called Virginia, where the first English colony in America was established the following year.

P. F. A.

DESOLATE
  BRENDON,
    June 1917.

CONTENTS

MAPS AND ILLUSTRATIONS

INTRODUCTION

There is much doubt as to when the first discovery of America by Europeans took place. It is, however, generally believed that the Norsemen, sailing from Greenland, reached the coasts of Labrador, Newfoundland, and Nova Scotia about the year 1000. These discoveries made no lasting impression on the mind of Europe, and the real discovery of America was not made until nearly five hundred years later.

From early in the fifteenth century the Portuguese had been steadily pushing their way down the coast of Africa in their attempts to open up a sea-route to India, and Portugal had become pre-eminent in the knowledge of geography. About the year 1470 Christopher Columbus, a native of Genoa, and his brother Bartholomew, settled in Lisbon. Here, ignorant of the existence of America and the Pacific Ocean, Columbus collected any information that was likely to help him in his projected voyage across the Atlantic. In 1484 his scheme for reaching China and India by sailing westwards was rejected by the Portuguese king. He then went to Spain, where he had to wait until the final conquest of the Moors at Granada in 1492, before he obtained the necessary assistance for his journey from Ferdinand and Isabella. In August of that year he set sail with three ships and discovered a number of islands, including Cuba and Hayti (Hispaniola), which

he believed were part of Asia, and which are still known
as the West Indies (the Indies reached by the westward
route).

In 1493 he again started on a second voyage with
a much larger fleet, and taking a more southerly course
than before, arrived once more at the West Indies.   In
this voyage the chief additional discovery that was
made was the island of Jamaica.   On a third voyage,
in 1498, he discovered Trinidad, and observed the
strong current of fresh water which came from the River
Orinoco.   Moreover he caught sight of the coast of
South America, though unaware that it was the mainland.   He set out on a fourth and last voyage in 1502–4
with the intention of sailing through the islands already
known to him and reaching Asia.   He arrived at the
mainland of Central America, and followed the coast of
Honduras as far south as the neighbourhood of Panama,
but added little to his previous discoveries.   Two years
after his return to Spain he died, still ignorant apparently that he had opened up a New World.   It was
reserved for others to prove the existence of the great
continent that blocked the way to the goal he sought.

One of Columbus's immediate successors was
Vicente Pinzon, who had sailed with him on his first
voyage.   On an expedition in 1499–1500 he reached
the shores of Brazil, discovered the mouth of the
Amazon, and surveyed 300 miles of the coast of South
America.   About three months later the coast of Brazil
was also reached by Cabral, a Portuguese, who was
making a voyage to the East by the Cape of Good Hope,
and was blown out of his course.   To this period belong
also the voyages of the Florentine, Amerigo Vespucci,
some in the service of Spain, and some in that of

Portugal. There is now grave doubt as to the accuracy of his statements, and in any case he achieved a fame far beyond his merits, since the new continent was named after him, America. Other explorers followed and its outline became gradually known. The voyage of Ponce de Leon led to the acquisition of Florida in 1512 by the Spaniards—their first possession in North America. Next year another Spaniard, Balboa, crossed the Isthmus of Panama and saw the Pacific. Then followed the conquest of Mexico and Peru by the Spaniards, and the gradual penetration of a large part of South and Central America.

To return to exploration further north. In the reign of Henry VII, John Cabot (like Columbus, a Genoese), who had settled in Bristol, made an attempt to find a north-west passage, and re-discovered in 1497 New-foundland and part of the coast of North America. In 1500–1501 a Portuguese, Cortereal, also reached Newfoundland, and these voyages opened up the famous fisheries, which attracted among others numbers of Frenchmen, especially Bretons. In 1524 Verazzano, a Florentine in the service of the King of France, started on a voyage in which he explored a considerable part of the coast of what afterwards became the United States.

This voyage of Verazzano opened the way to a French settlement in Florida, but the beginning of French colonization on a large scale in America was due to the voyages of Jacques Cartier between 1534 and 1543, in which he explored the Gulf of St Lawrence and the River St Lawrence as far as Montreal; and the information he gathered led afterwards to the foundation of the French colony of Canada.

The first Englishman who sailed along the coast of the United States was Sir John Hawkins in 1565. The first English colonizing expedition was that of Sir Humfrey Gilbert in 1583. He sailed to Newfoundland, where he took possession of St Johns and the neighbourhood, but owing to various mishaps did nothing further, and was lost with his ship on the return voyage. His half-brother, Sir Walter Ralegh, who was keenly interested in schemes of colonization, sent another expedition under Amadas and Barlow in the following year, 1584, with directions to sail by the Southern route past the Canaries and to take possession of land between Florida and Newfoundland. To this land (afterwards North Carolina) Queen Elizabeth gave the name of Virginia, and next year the first English colony in America was established here. This proved a failure, and it was not until the year 1607 that the first permanent colony was founded. It was named Jamestown, and was also in Virginia, but further north than the original settlement.

NOTE. Columbus's Voyages are taken from Major's *Select Letters of Columbus* (Hakluyt Society, 1847), and the extracts from the journal are, by kind permission of the Hakluyt Society, from Markham's *Journal of the First Voyage of Columbus*. This translation is made from Las Casas' abridgment of Columbus's Journal, which is no longer in existence. He frequently quotes, however, the exact words of the original. The remaining voyages are from Hakluyt's *Principal Navigations*, etc.

SOME IMPORTANT DATES IN THE HISTORY OF DISCOVERY

1498.   Columbus (3rd voyage) discovers Trinidad and the Orinoco.

1499.   Amerigo Vespucci discovers Venezuela (though great doubt is now cast on the accuracy of his statements).

1500.   Pedro Cabral discovers Brazil.

1511.   Serrano reaches the Moluccas (the Spice Islands).

1513.   Balboa crosses the Isthmus of Panama, and sees the Pacific.

1519.   Cortez conquers Mexico.

1519.   Magellan starts on the first voyage round the world.

1520.   Magellan sails past Monte Video, Patagonia, and Tierra del Fuego, through his strait, and across the Pacific.

1521.   Magellan discovers the Ladrones, and is killed on the Philippines.

1522.   Sebastian del Cano, in Magellan's ship, *Victoria*, reaches Spain.

1531.   Pizarro conquers Peru.

1534.   Cartier explores the St Lawrence.

1541.   Orellana explores the Amazon.

1553.   Sir Hugh Willoughby attempts the North-East Passage, and sees Novaya Zemlya.

1554.   Chancellor, Willoughby's pilot, reaches Archangel, and travels thence to Moscow.

1558.   Jenkinson travels from Moscow to Bokhara.

1576.   Martin Frobisher discovers his bay.

1577–1580.   Drake sails round the world—the first Englishman who does this.

1586–88.   Cavendish sails round the world.

1586.   Davis sails through his strait.

1596.   Barents discovers Spitzbergen.

1605.   Torres discovers his strait.

1608.   Champlain discovers Lake Ontario.

1610.   Hudson sails through his strait into his bay.

1616.   Lemaire rounds Cape Horn (Hoorn, named after the town to which his ships belonged).

1616. Baffin discovers his bay.

1642. Tasman discovers Van Diemen's Land (Tasmania) and Staaten Land (New Zealand).

1699. Dampier discovers his strait.

1768–71. Cook (1st voyage) re-discovers New Zealand and discovers east coast of New Holland (Australia).

1770. Bruce discovers the source of the Blue Nile.

1776–79. Cook (3rd voyage) discovers the Sandwich Islands.

1785–88. La Pérouse explores N.E. coasts of Asia, the China and Japan Seas, and discovers Saghalien.

1789–93. Mackenzie discovers his river and British Columbia.

1792. Vancouver explores his island.

1796. Mungo Park reaches the Niger.

1797. Bass discovers his strait.

1799–1804. Humboldt explores South America.

1801–4. Flinders surveys the south coast of Australia.

1819–22. Franklin, Back and Richardson attempt the North-West Passage by land.

1819. Parry discovers Lancaster Sound.

1822. Denham and Clapperton discover Lake Tchad.

1828–31. Sturt traces the Darling and Murray Rivers.

1829–33. Ross attempts the North-West Passage, and discovers Boothia.

1840–42. Ross explores the Antarctic, and discovers Victoria Land, and the volcanoes Erebus and Terror (named after his ships).

1845–47. Franklin's last voyage.

1849–56. Livingstone explores the Zambesi, and discovers the Victoria Falls.

1850–54. M'Clure succeeds in the North-West Passage.

1858. Burton and Speke discover Lake Tanganyika, and Speke discovers Victoria Nyanza.

1858–62. Stuart crosses Australia from south to north.

1858–64. Livingstone explores Lake Nyasa.

1864. Baker discovers Albert Nyanza.

1867. Livingstone discovers Lake Moero.

1874–5. Cameron crosses equatorial Africa.

1876–7. Stanley explores the Congo River, and opens up Central Africa.

1878–79. Nordenskiöld succeeds in the North-East Passage.

1887–89. Stanley's expedition to rescue Emin Pasha. He discovers the Pigmies, and the Ruwenzori (the Mountains of the Moon).

1893–97. Nansen's voyage across the Arctic Ocean in the *Fram*. He reaches farthest north (86° 14′).

1909. Peary reaches the North Pole.

1911. Amundsen reaches the South Pole.

1912. Scott reaches the South Pole.

COLUMBUS. FIRST VOYAGE (1492–1493)

I

A letter addressed to the noble Lord Raphael Sanchez,
Treasurer to their most invincible Majesties, Ferdinand and Isabella, King and Queen of Spain, by
Christopher Columbus, to whom our age is greatly
indebted, treating of the islands of India recently
discovered beyond the Ganges, to explore which
he had been sent eight months before under the
auspices and at the expense of their said Majesties.

Knowing that it will afford you pleasure to learn
that I have brought my undertaking to a successful
termination, I have decided upon writing you this letter
to acquaint you with all the events which have occurred
in my voyage, and the discoveries which have resulted
from it.   Thirty-three days after my departure from
Cadiz I reached the Indian sea, where I discovered
many islands, thickly peopled, of which I took possession without resistance in the name of our most illus-
trious Monarch, by public proclamation and with un-
furled banners.   To the first of these islands, which
is called by the Indians Guanahani, I gave the name of
the blessed Saviour (San Salvador), relying upon whose
protection I had reached this as well as the other islands ;
to each of these I also gave a name, ordering that one
should be called Santa Maria de la Concepcion, another

Fernandina, the third Isabella, the fourth Juana, and so with all the rest respectively. As soon as we arrived at that, which as I have said was named Juana, I proceeded along its coast a short distance westward, and found it to be so large and apparently without termination, that I could not suppose it to be an island, but the continental province of Cathay. Seeing, however, no towns or populous places on the sea coast, but only a few detached houses and cottages, with whose inhabitants I was unable to communicate, because they fled as soon as they saw us, I went further on, thinking that in my progress I should certainly find some city or village. At length, after proceeding a great way and finding that nothing new presented itself, and that the line of coast was leading us northwards (which I wished to avoid, because it was winter, and it was my intention to move southwards; and because moreover the winds were contrary), I resolved not to attempt any further progress, but rather to turn back and retrace my course to a certain bay that I had observed, and from which I afterwards dispatched two of our men to ascertain whether there were a king or any cities in that province. These men reconnoitred the country for three days, and found a most numerous population, and great numbers of houses, though small, and built without any regard to order: with which information they returned to us. In the mean time I had learned from some Indians whom I had seized, that that country was certainly an island: and therefore I sailed towards the east, coasting to the distance of three hundred and twenty-two miles, which brought us to the extremity of it; from this point I saw lying eastwards another island, fifty-four miles distant from Juana, to which

A ship of Columbus's fleet

I gave the name of Española: I went thither, and
steered my course eastward as I had done at Juana,
even to the distance of five hundred and sixty-four
miles along the north coast.   This said island of Juana
is exceedingly fertile, as indeed are all the others; it
is surrounded with many bays, spacious, very secure,
and surpassing any that I have ever seen; numerous
large and healthful rivers intersect it, and it also contains
many very lofty mountains.   All these islands are
very beautiful, and distinguished by a diversity of
scenery; they are filled with a great variety of trees
of immense height, and which I believe to retain their
foliage in all seasons; for when I saw them they were
as verdant and luxuriant as they usually are in Spain
in the month of May,—some of them were blossoming,
some bearing fruit, and all flourishing in the greatest
perfection, according to their respective stages of growth,
and the nature and quality of each: yet the islands are
not so thickly wooded as to be impassable.   The night-
ingale and various birds were singing in countless
numbers, and that in November, the month in which
I arrived there.   There are besides in the same island
of Juana seven or eight kinds of palm trees, which,
like all the other trees, herbs, and fruits, considerably
surpass ours in height and beauty.   The pines also
are very handsome, and there are very extensive fields
and meadows, a variety of birds, different kinds of
honey, and many sorts of metals, but no iron.   In
that island also which I have before said we named
Española, there are mountains of very great size and
beauty, vast plains, groves, and very fruitful fields,
admirably adapted for tillage, pasture, and habitation.
The convenience and excellence of the harbours in

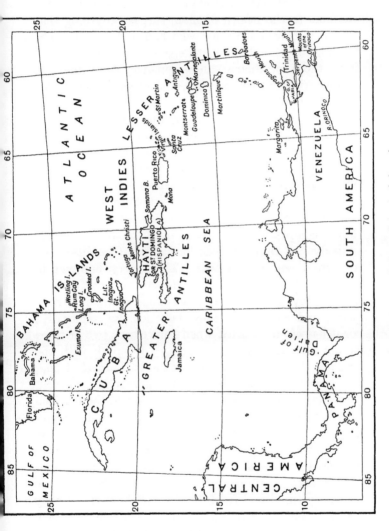

West Indies, and part of the mainland of America

this island, and the abundance of the rivers, so indis-
pensable to the health of man, surpass anything that
would be believed by one who had not seen it.   The
trees, herbage, and fruits of Española are very different
from those of Juana, and moreover it abounds in
various kinds of spices, gold, and other metals.   The
inhabitants of both sexes in this island, and in all the
others which I have seen, or of which I have received
information, go always naked as they were born, with
the exception of some of the women, who use the
covering of a leaf, or small bough, or an apron of cotton
which they prepare for that purpose.   None of them,
as I have already said, are possessed of any iron, neither
have they weapons, being unacquainted with, and indeed incompetent to use them, not from any deformity
of body (for they are well-formed), but because they
are timid and full of fear.   They carry however in
lieu of arms, canes dried in the sun, on the ends of
which they fix heads of dried wood sharpened to a
point, and even these they dare not use habitually;
for it has often occurred when I have sent two or three
of my men to any of the villages to speak with the
natives, that they have come out in a disorderly troop,
and have fled in such haste at the approach of our men,
that the fathers forsook their children and the children
their fathers.   This timidity did not arise from any
loss or injury that they had received from us; for, on
the contrary, I gave to all I approached whatever
articles I had about me, such as cloth and many other
things, taking nothing of theirs in return : but they are
naturally timid and fearful.   As soon however as they
see that they are safe, and have laid aside all fear, they
are very simple and honest, and exceedingly liberal

Columbus landing in Hispaniola

with all they have; none of them refusing any thing
he may possess when he is asked for it, but on the contrary inviting us to ask them. They exhibit great
love towards all others in preference to themselves:
they also give objects of great value for trifles, and content themselves with very little or nothing in return.
I however forbad that these trifles and articles of no
value (such as pieces of dishes, plates, and glass, keys,
and leather straps) should be given to them, although
if they could obtain them, they imagined themselves
to be possessed of the most beautiful trinkets in the
world. It even happened that a sailor received for
a leather strap as much gold as was worth three golden
nobles, and for things of more trifling value offered by
our men, especially newly-coined blancas, or any gold
coins, the Indians would give whatever the seller required; as, for instance, an ounce and a half or two
ounces of gold, or thirty or forty pounds of cotton,
with which commodity they were already acquainted.
Thus they bartered, like idiots, cotton and gold for
fragments of bows, glasses, bottles, and jars; which
I forbad as being unjust, and myself gave them many
beautiful and acceptable articles which I had brought
with me, taking nothing from them in return; I did
this in order that I might the more easily conciliate
them, that they might be led to become Christians,
and be inclined to entertain a regard for the King and
Queen, our Princes and all Spaniards, and that I might
induce them to take an interest in seeking out, and
collecting, and delivering to us such things as they
possessed in abundance, but which we greatly needed.
They practise no kind of idolatry, but have a firm belief
that all strength and power, and indeed all good things,

are in heaven, and that I had descended from thence with these ships and sailors, and under this impression was I received after they had thrown aside their fears. Nor are they slow or stupid, but of very clear understanding; and those men who have crossed to the neighbouring islands give an admirable description of everything they observed; but they never saw any people clothed, nor any ships like ours. On my arrival at that sea, I had taken some Indians by force from the first island that I came to, in order that they might learn our language, and communicate to us what they knew respecting the country; which plan succeeded excellently, and was a great advantage to us, for in a short time, either by gestures and signs, or by words, we were enabled to understand each other. These men are still travelling with me, and although they have been with us now a long time, they continue to entertain the idea that I have descended from heaven; and on our arrival at any new place they published this, crying out immediately with a loud voice to the other Indians, "Come, come and look upon beings of a celestial race": upon which both women and men, children and adults, young men and old, when they got rid of the fear they at first entertained, would come out in throngs, crowding the roads to see us, some bringing food, others drink, with astonishing affection and kindness. Each of these islands has a great number of canoes, built of solid wood, narrow and not unlike our double-banked boats in length and shape, but swifter in their motion: they steer them only by the oar. These canoes are of various sizes, but the greater number are constructed with eighteen banks of oars, and with these they cross to the other

islands, which are of countless number, to carry on
traffic with the people. I saw some of these canoes
that held as many as seventy-eight rowers. In all
these islands there is no difference of physiognomy, of
manners, or of language, but they all clearly understand each other, a circumstance very propitious for
the realization of what I conceive to be the principal
wish of our most serene King, namely, the conversion
of these people to the holy faith of Christ, to which
indeed, as far as I can judge, they are very favourable
and well-disposed. I said before, that I went three
hundred and twenty-two miles in a direct line from
west to east, along the coast of the island of Juana;
judging by which voyage, and the length of the passage,
I can assert that it is larger than England and Scotland
united; for independent of the said three hundred and
twenty-two miles, there are in the western part of the
island two provinces which I did not visit; one of these
is called by the Indians Anam, and its inhabitants are
born with tails. These provinces extend to a hundred
and fifty-three miles in length, as I have learnt from the
Indians whom I have brought with me, and who are
well acquainted with the country. But the extent
of Española is greater than all Spain from Catalonia
to Fontarabia, which is easily proved, because one of
its four sides which I myself coasted in a direct line,
from west to east, measures five hundred and forty
miles. This island is to be regarded with especial
interest, and not to be slighted; for although as I have
said I took possession of all these islands in the name
of our invincible King, and the government of them
is unreservedly committed to his said Majesty, yet there
was one large town in Española of which especially I

took possession, situated in a remarkably favourable spot, and in every way convenient for the purposes of gain and commerce. To this town I gave the name of Navidad del Señor, and ordered a fortress to be built there, which must by this time be completed, in which I left as many men as I thought necessary, with all sorts of arms, and enough provisions for more than a year. I also left them one caravel, and skilful workmen both in ship-building and other arts, and engaged the favour and friendship of the King of the island in their behalf, to a degree that would not be believed, for these people are so amiable and friendly that even the King took a pride in calling me his brother. But supposing their feelings should become changed, and they should wish to injure those who have remained in the fortress, they could not do so, for they have no arms, they go naked, and are moreover too cowardly; so that those who hold the said fortress can easily keep the whole island in check, without any pressing danger to themselves, provided they do not transgress the directions and regulations which I have given them. As far as I have learned, every man throughout these islands is united to but one wife, with the exception of the kings and princes, who are allowed to have twenty: the women seem to work more than the men. I could not clearly understand whether the people possess any private property, for I observed that one man had the charge of distributing various things to the rest, but especially meat and provisions and the like. I did not find, as some of us had expected, any cannibals amongst them, but on the contrary men of great deference and kindness. Neither are they black, like the Ethiopians: their hair is smooth and straight:

for they do not dwell where the rays of the sun strike most vividly,—and the sun has intense power there, the distance from the equinoctial line being, it appears, but six-and-twenty degrees. On the tops of the mountains the cold is very great, but the effect of this upon the Indians is lessened by their being accustomed to the climate, and by their frequently indulging in the use of very hot meats and drinks. Thus, as I have already said, I saw no cannibals, nor did I hear of any, except in a certain island called Charis, which is the second from Española on the side towards India, where dwell a people who are considered by the neighbouring islanders as most ferocious: and these feed upon human flesh. The same people have many kinds of canoes, in which they cross to all the surrounding islands and rob and plunder wherever they can; they are not different from the other islanders, except that they wear their hair long, like women, and make use of the bows and javelins of cane, with sharpened spear-points fixed on the thickest end, which I have before described, and therefore they are looked upon as ferocious, and regarded by the other Indians with unbounded fear; but I think no more of them than of the rest. These are the men who form unions with certain women, who dwell alone in the island Matenin, which lies next to Española on the side towards India; these latter employ themselves in no labour suitable to their own sex, for they use bows and javelins like those I have already described, and for defensive armour have plates of brass, of which metal they possess great abundance. They assure me that there is another island larger than Española, whose inhabit-ants have no hair, and which abounds in gold more

than any of the rest. I bring with me individuals of
this island and of the others that I have seen, who are
proofs of the facts which I state. Finally, to compress
into few words the entire summary of my voyage and
speedy return, and of the advantages derivable there-
from, I promise, that with a little assistance afforded
me by our most invincible sovereigns, I will procure
them as much gold as they need, as great a quantity
of spices, of cotton, and of mastic (which is only found
in Chios), and as many men for the service of the navy
as their Majesties may require. I promise also rhubarb
and other sorts of drugs, which I am persuaded the
men whom I have left in the aforesaid fortress have
found already and will continue to find; for I myself
have tarried nowhere longer than I was compelled to
do by the winds, except in the city of Navidad, while
I provided for the building of the fortress, and took
the necessary precautions for the perfect security of
the men I left there. Although all I have related
may appear to be wonderful and unheard of, yet the
results of my voyage would have been more astonishing if I had had at my disposal such ships as I required.
But these great and marvellous results are not to be
attributed to any merit of mine, but to the holy Christian faith, and to the piety and religion of our Sovereigns; for that which the unaided intellect of man
could not compass, the spirit of God has granted to
human exertions, for God is wont to hear the prayers
of his servants who love his precepts even to the per-
formance of apparent impossibilities. Thus it has
happened to me in the present instance, who have
accomplished a task to which the powers of mortal
men had never hitherto attained; for if there have been

those who have anywhere written or spoken of these islands, they have done so with doubts and conjectures, and no one has ever asserted that he has seen them, on which account their writings have been looked upon as little else than fables.   Therefore let the king and queen, our princes and their most happy kingdoms, and all the other provinces of Christendom, render thanks to our Lord and Saviour Jesus Christ, who has granted us so great a victory and such prosperity. Let processions be made, and sacred feasts be held, and the temples be adorned with festive boughs.   Let Christ rejoice on earth, as he rejoices in heaven in the prospect of the salvation of the souls of so many nations hitherto lost.   Let us also rejoice, as well on account of the exaltation of our faith, as on account of the increase of our temporal prosperity, of which not only Spain, but all Christendom will be partakers.

Such are the events which I have briefly described. Farewell.

Lisbon, the 14th of March.

CHRISTOPHER COLUMBUS,
Admiral of the Fleet of the Ocean.

II

EXTRACTS FROM THE JOURNAL OF THE FIRST VOYAGE OF COLUMBUS

PROLOGUE AND DEPARTURE

In the name of our Lord Jesus Christ.

Because, O most Christian, and very high, very excellent, and puissant Princes, King and Queen of the Spains and of the islands of the Sea, our Lords, in this present year of 1492, after your Highnesses had given an end to the war with the Moors who reigned in Europe, and had finished it in the very great city of Granada, where in this present year, on the second day of the month of January, by force of arms, I saw the royal banners of your Highnesses placed on the towers of Alhambra, which is the fortress of that city, and I saw the Moorish King come forth from the gates of the city and kiss the royal hands of your Highnesses, and of the Prince my Lord, and presently in that same month, acting on the information that I had given to your Highnesses touching the lands of India, and respecting a Prince who is called *Gran Can*, which means in our language King of Kings, how he and his ancestors had sent to Rome many times to ask for learned men of our holy faith to teach him, and how the Holy Father had never complied, insomuch that many people believing in idolatries were lost by receiving doctrine of perdition: YOUR HIGHNESSES, as Catholic Christians and Princes who love the holy Christian faith, and the propagation of it, and who are enemies to the sect of Mahomet and to all idolatries and heresies, resolved to send me, Cristobal Colon, to the said parts of India to see the said princes, and the cities and lands, and their disposition, with a view that they might be converted to our holy faith; and ordered that I should not go by land to the eastward, as had been customary, but that I should go by way of the west, whither up to this day, we do not know for certain that any one has gone.

Thus, after having turned out all the Jews from all your kingdoms and lordships, in the same month of January, your Highnesses gave orders to me that with a sufficient fleet I should go to the said parts of India, and for this they made great concessions to me, and ennobled me, so that henceforward I should be called Don, and should be Chief Admiral of the Ocean Sea, perpetual Viceroy and Governor of all the islands and continents that I should discover and gain, and that I might hereafter discover and gain in the Ocean Sea, and that my eldest son should succeed, and so on from generation to generation for ever.

I left the city of Granada on the 12th day of May, in the same year of 1492, being Saturday, and came to the town of Palos, which is a seaport; where I equipped three vessels well suited for such service; and departed from that port, well supplied with provisions and with many sailors, on the 3rd day of August of the same year, being Friday, half an hour before sunrise, taking the route to the islands of Canaria, belonging to your Highnesses, which are in the said Ocean Sea, that I might thence take my departure for navigating until I should arrive at the Indies, and give the letters of your Highnesses to those princes, so as to comply with my orders. As part of my duty I thought it well to write an account of all the voyage very punctually, noting from day to day all that I should do and see, and that should happen, as will be seen further on. Also, Lords Princes, I resolved to

Parting of Columbus with Ferdinand and Isabella

describe each night what passed in the day, and to note each day how I navigated at night. I propose to construct a new chart for navigating, on which I shall delineate all the sea and lands of the Ocean in their proper positions under their bearings; and further,

I propose to prepare a book, and to put down all as it were in a picture, by latitude from the equator, and western longitude. Above all, I shall have accomplished much, for I shall forget sleep, and shall work at the business of navigation, that so the service may be performed; all which will entail great labour.

[After leaving the Canaries Columbus kept two reckonings, one correct, and one for the crew, in which he entered less than the actual distances run, to make the voyage appear shorter, so that they should not be disheartened. From September 14 onwards they saw signs, such as birds and tufts of floating grass, which made them think that land was near. On Tuesday, September 25, they thought they saw land, and all said the *Gloria in excelsis*. This, however, turned out to be clouds.]

Land Discovered

Thursday, 11th of October.

The course was W.S.W., and there was more sea than there had been during the whole of the voyage. They saw sandpipers, and a green reed near the ship. Those of the caravel *Pinta* saw a cane and a pole, and they took up another small pole which appeared to have been worked with iron; also another bit of cane, a land-plant, and a small board. The crew of the caravel *Niña* also saw signs of land, and a small branch covered with berries. Everyone breathed afresh and rejoiced at these signs. The run until sunset was 26 leagues.

After sunset the Admiral returned to his original west course, and they went along at the rate of 12 miles an hour. Up to two hours after midnight they had gone 90 miles, equal to 22½ leagues. As the caravel *Pinta* was a better sailer, and went ahead of the Admiral, she found the land, and made the signals ordered by the Admiral. The land was first seen by a sailor named Rodrigo de Triana. But the Admiral, at ten in the previous night, being on the castle of the poop, saw a light, though it was so uncertain that he could not affirm it was land. He called Pedro Gutierrez, a gentleman of the King's bedchamber, and said that there seemed to be a light, and that he should look at it. He did so, and saw it. The Admiral said the same to Rodrigo Sanchez of Segovia, whom the King and Queen had sent with the fleet as inspector, but he could see nothing, because he was not in a place whence anything could be seen. After the Admiral had spoken he saw the light once or twice, and it was like a wax candle rising and falling. It seemed to few to be an indication of land; but the Admiral made certain that land was close. When they said the *Salve*, which all the sailors were accustomed to sing in their way, the Admiral asked and admonished the men to keep a good look-out on the forecastle, and to watch well for land; and to him who should first cry out that he saw land, he would give a silk doublet, besides the other rewards promised by the Sovereigns, which were 10,000 maravedis to him who should first see it. At two hours after midnight the land was sighted at a distance of two leagues. They shortened sail, and lay by under the mainsail without the bonnets. The vessels were hove to, waiting for daylight; and on Friday they arrived at a small island of the Lucayos, called, in the language of the Indians, *Guanahani*. Presently they saw naked people.

The Admiral went on shore in the armed boat, and Martin Alonso Pinzon, and Vicente Yañez, his brother, who was captain of the *Niña*. The Admiral took the royal standard, and the captains went with two banners of the green cross, which the Admiral took in all the ships as a sign, with an F and a Y and a crown over each letter, one on one side of the cross and the other on the other. Having landed, they saw trees very green, and much water, and fruits of diverse kinds. The Admiral called to the two captains, and to the others who leaped on shore, and to Rodrigo Escovedo, secretary of the whole fleet, and to Rodrigo Sanchez of Segovia, and said that they should bear faithful testimony that he, in presence of all, had taken, as he now took, possession of the said island for the King and for the Queen, his Lords making the declarations that are required, as is more largely set forth in the testimonies which were then made in writing.

Presently many inhabitants of the island assembled. What follows is in the actual words of the Admiral in his book of the first navigation and discovery of the Indies. "I," he says, "that we might form great friendship, for I knew that they were a people who could be more easily freed and converted to our holy faith by love than by force, gave to some of them red caps, and glass beads to put round their necks, and many other things of little value, which gave them great pleasure, and made them so much our friends that it was a marvel to see. They afterwards came to the ship's boats where we were, swimming and bringing us parrots, cotton threads in skeins, darts, and many other things; and we exchanged them for other things that we gave them, such as glass beads

and small bells.   In fine, they took all, and gave what
they had with good will.   It appeared to me to be
a race of people very poor in everything.   They go
as naked as when their mothers bore them, and so do
the women, although I did not see more than one young
girl.   All I saw were youths, none more than thirty
years of age.   They are very well made, with very
handsome bodies, and very good countenances.   Their
hair is short and coarse, almost like the hairs of a
horse's tail.   They wear the hairs brought down to
the eyebrows, except a few locks behind, which they
wear long and never cut.   They paint themselves
black, and they are the colour of the Canarians, neither
black nor white.   Some paint themselves white, others
red, and others of what colour they find.   Some paint
their faces, others the whole body, some only round
the eyes, others only on the nose.   They neither carry
nor know anything of arms, for I showed them swords,
and they took them by the blade and cut themselves
through ignorance.   They have no iron, their darts being
wands without iron, some of them having a fish's tooth
at the end, and others being pointed in various ways.
They are all of fair stature and size, with good faces,
and well made.   I saw some with marks of wounds on
their bodies, and I made signs to ask what it was, and
they gave me to understand that people from other
adjacent islands came with the intention of seizing
them, and that they defended themselves.   I believed,
and still believe, that they come here from the mainland to take them prisoners.   They should be good
servants and intelligent, for I observed that they
quickly took in what was said to them, and I believe
that they would easily be made Christians, as it

appeared to me that they had no religion. I, our Lord
being pleased, will take hence, at the time of my departure, six natives for your Highnesses, that they may
learn to speak. I saw no beast of any kind except
parrots, on this island." The above is in the words
of the Admiral.

Saturday, 13th of October.

" As soon as dawn broke many of these people came
to the beach, all youths, as I have said, and all of good
stature, a very handsome people. Their hair is not
curly, but loose and coarse, like horse hair. In all the
forehead is broad, more so than in any other people
I have hitherto seen. Their eyes are very beautiful
and not small, and themselves far from black, but the
colour of the Canarians. Nor should anything else
be expected, as this island is in a line east and west
from the island of Hierro in the Canaries. Their legs
are very straight, all in one line, and no belly, but very
well formed. They came to the ship in small canoes,
made out of the trunk of a tree like a long boat, and
all of one piece, and wonderfully worked, considering
the country. They are large, some of them holding
40 to 45 men, others smaller, and some only large
enough to hold one man. They are propelled with a
paddle like a baker's shovel, and go at a marvellous
rate. If the canoe capsizes they all promptly begin
to swim, and to bale it out with calabashes that they
take with them. They brought skeins of cotton
thread, parrots, darts, and other small things which
it would be tedious to recount, and they give all in
exchange for anything that may be given to them.
I was attentive, and took trouble to ascertain if there

was gold. I saw that some of them had a small piece fastened in a hole they have in the nose, and by signs I was able to make out that to the south, or going from the island to the south, there was a king who had great cups full, and who possessed a great quantity. I tried to get them to go there, but afterwards I saw that they had no inclination. I resolved to wait until to-morrow in the afternoon and then to depart, shaping a course to the S.W., for, according to what many of them told me, there was land to the S., to the S.W., and N.W., and that the natives from the N.W. often came to attack them, and went on to the S.W. in search of gold and precious stones.

"This island is rather large and very flat, with bright green trees, much water, and a very large lake in the centre, without any mountain, and the whole land so green that it is a pleasure to look on it. The people are very docile, and for the longing to possess our things, and not having anything to give in return, they take what they can get, and presently swim away. Still, they give away all they have got, for whatever may be given to them, down to broken bits of crockery and glass. I saw one give 16 skeins of cotton for three *ceotis* of Portugal, equal to one *blanca* of Spain, the skeins being as much as an *arroba* of cotton thread. 1 shall keep it, and shall allow no one to take it, preserving it all for your Highnesses, for it may be obtained in abundance. It is grown in this island, though the short time did not admit of my ascertaining this for a certainty. Here also is found the gold they wear fastened in their noses. But, in order not to lose time, I intend to go and see if I can find the island of Cipango. Now, as it is night, all the natives have gone on shore with their canoes."

Sunday, 14th of October.

"At dawn I ordered the ship's boat and the boats of the caravels to be got ready, and I went along the coast of the island to the N.N.E., to see the other side, which was on the other side to the east, and also to see the villages. Presently I saw two or three, and the people all came to the shore, calling out and giving thanks to God. Some of them brought us water, others came with food, and when they saw that I did not want to land, they got into the sea, and came swimming to us. We understood that they asked us if we had come from heaven. One old man came into the boat, and others cried out, in loud voices, to all the men and women, to come and see the men who had come from heaven, and to bring them to eat and drink. Many came, including women, each bringing something, giving thanks to God, throwing themselves on the ground and shouting to us to come on shore. But I was afraid to land, seeing an extensive reef of rocks which surrounded the island, with deep water between it and the shore forming a port large enough for as many ships as there are in Christendom, but with a very narrow entrance. It is true that within this reef there are some sunken rocks, but the sea has no more motion than the water in a well. In order to see all this I went this morning, that I might be able to give a full account to your Highnesses, and also where a fortress might be established. I saw a piece of land which appeared like an island, although it is not one, and on it there were six houses. It might be converted into an island in two days, though I do not see that it would be necessary, for these people are very simple as regards the use of arms, as your Highnesses will see from the seven that I caused to be taken, to bring home and learn our language and return; unless your Highnesses should order them all to be brought to Castille, or to be kept as captives on the same island; for with fifty men they can all be subjugated and made to do what is required of them. Close to the above peninsula there are gardens of the most beautiful trees I ever saw, and with leaves as green as those of Castille in the months of April and May, and much water. I examined all that port, and afterwards I returned to the ship and made sail."

[They then visited the islands Santa Maria de la Concepcion (Rum Cay), Fernandina (Long Island), and arrived at Isabella (Crooked Island).]

THE ISLAND OF ISABELLA

Sunday, 21st of October.

"At ten o'clock I arrived here, off this islet, and anchored, as well as the caravels. After breakfast I went on shore, and found only one house, in which there was no one, and I supposed they had fled from fear, because all their property was left in the house. I would not allow anything to be touched, but set out with the captains and people to explore the island. If the others already seen are very beautiful, green, and fertile, this is much more so, with large trees and very green. Here there are large lagoons with wonderful vegetation on their banks. Throughout the island all is green, and the herbage like April in Andalusia. The songs of the birds were so pleasant that it seemed as if a man could never wish to leave the place. The

flocks of parrots concealed the sun; and the birds were
so numerous, and of so many different kinds, that it
was wonderful. There are trees of a thousand sorts,
and all have their several fruits; and I feel the most
unhappy man in the world not to know them, for I am
well assured that they are all valuable. I bring home
specimens of them, and also of the land. Thus walking along round one of the lakes I saw a serpent, which
we killed, and I bring home the skin for your Highnesses.
As soon as it saw us it went into the lagoon, and we
followed, as the water was not very deep, until we
killed it with lances. It is 7 *palmos* long, and I believe
that there are many like it in these lagoons. Here
I came upon some aloes, and I have determined to
take ten quintals on board to-morrow, for they tell
me that they are worth a good deal. Also, while in
search of good water, we came to a village about half
a league from our anchorage. The people, as soon
as they heard us, all fled and left their houses, hiding
their property in the wood. I would not allow a thing
to be touched, even the value of a pin. Presently
some men among them came to us, and one came quite
close. I gave him some bells and glass beads, which
made him very content and happy. That our friendship might be further increased, I resolved to ask him
for something; I requested him to get some water.
After I had gone on board, the natives came to the
beach with calabashes full of water, and they delighted
much in giving it to us. I ordered another string of
glass beads to be presented to them, and they said
they would come again to-morrow. I wished to fill
up all the ships with water at this place, and, if there
should be time, I intended to search the island until

I had had speech with the king, and seen whether he had the gold of which I had heard. I shall then shape a course for another much larger island, which I believe to be Cipango, judging from the signs made by the Indians I bring with me. They call it *Cuba*, and they say that there are ships and many skilful sailors there. Beyond this island there is another called *Bosio*, which they also say is very large, and others we shall see as we pass, lying between. According as I obtain tidings of gold or spices I shall settle what should be done. I am still resolved to go to the mainland and the city of Guisay, and to deliver the letters of your Highnesses to the Gran Can, requesting a reply and returning with it."

[Thence they sailed to Cuba, and explored part of the north coast. At one place Columbus, believing that he had reached the mainland of China, sent two Spaniards and two Indians to collect information, and to ask for the king of that land, with instructions to return in six days.]

REPORT OF THE ENVOYS. TOBACCO AND COTTON

Tuesday, 6th of November.

"Yesterday, at night," says the Admiral, "the two men came back who had been sent to explore the interior. They said that after walking 12 leagues they came to a village of 50 houses, where there were a thousand inhabitants, for many live in one house. These houses are like very large booths. They said that they were received with great solemnity, according to custom, and all, both men and women, came out to see them. They were lodged in the best houses, and the

people touched them, kissing their hands and feet,
marvelling and believing that they came from heaven,
and so they gave them to understand. They gave
them to eat of what they had. When they arrived,
the chief people conducted them by the arms to the
principal house, gave them two chairs on which to sit,
and all the natives sat round them on the ground.
The Indian who came with them described the manner
of living of the Christians, and said that they were good
people. Presently the men went out, and the women
came sitting round them in the same way, kissing their
hands and feet, and looking to see if they were of flesh
and bones like themselves. They begged the Spaniards
to remain with them at least five days." The Spaniards
showed the natives specimens of cinnamon, pepper,
and other spices which the Admiral had given them,
and they said, by signs, that there was plenty at a
short distance from thence to S.E., but that there
they did not know whether there was any. Finding
that they had no information respecting cities, the
Spaniards returned; and if they had desired to take
those who wished to accompany them, more than 500
men and women would have come, because they thought
the Spaniards were returning to heaven. There came,
however, a principal man of the village and his son,
with a servant. The Admiral conversed with them,
and showed them much honour. They made signs
respecting many lands and islands in those parts.
The Admiral thought of bringing them to the Sovereigns.
He says that he knew not what fancy took them; either
from fear, or owing to the dark night, they wanted to
land. The ship was at the time high and dry, but
not wishing to make them angry, he let them go, on

their saying that they would return at dawn, but they never came back. The two Christians met with many people on the road going home, men and women with a half-burnt weed in their hands, being the herbs they are accustomed to smoke. They did not find villages on the road of more than five houses, all receiving them with the same reverence. They saw many kinds of trees, herbs, and sweet-smelling flowers; and birds of many different kinds, unlike those of Spain, except the partridges, geese, of which there are many, and singing nightingales. They saw no quadrupeds except the dogs that do not bark. The land is very fertile, and is cultivated with yams and several kinds of beans different from ours, as well as corn. There were great quantities of cotton gathered, spun, and worked up.

[On November 21, Martin Alonso Pinzon in the *Pinta* parted company with the other two ships "in disobedience to and against the wish of the Admiral, and out of avarice, thinking that an Indian who had been put on board his caravel could show him where there was much gold. So he parted company, not owing to bad weather, but because he chose."

From Cuba Columbus sailed to Española (Hayti), and along the north coast, hoping to find gold mines.

A friendly chief, Guacanagari, invited the Admiral to come with the ships to his land, where he would give him all he wanted.]

Wreck of the Flag-ship

Tuesday, 25th of December.   Christmas.

Navigating yesterday, with little wind, from *Santo Tome* to *Punta Santa*, and being a league from it, at about eleven o'clock at night the Admiral went down to get some sleep, for he had not had any rest for two days and a night. As it was calm, the sailor who steered the ship thought he would go to sleep, leaving the tiller in charge of a boy. The Admiral had forbidden this throughout the voyage, whether it was blowing or whether it was calm. The boys were never to be entrusted with the helm. The Admiral had no anxiety respecting sand-banks and rocks, because, when he sent the boats to that king on Sunday, they had passed to the east of *Punta Santa* at least three leagues and a half, and the sailors had seen all the coast, and the rocks there are from *Punta Santa*, for a distance of three leagues to the E.S.E. They saw the course that should be taken, which had not been the case before, during this voyage. It pleased our Lord that, at twelve o'clock at night, when the Admiral had retired to rest, and when all had fallen asleep, seeing that it was a dead calm and the sea like glass, the tiller being in the hands of a boy, the current carried the ship on one of the sand-banks. If it had not been night the bank could have been seen, and the surf on it could be heard for a good league. But the ship ran upon it so gently that it could scarcely be felt. The boy, who felt the helm and heard the rush of the sea, cried out. The Admiral at once came up, and so quickly that no one had felt that the ship was aground. Presently the master of the ship, whose watch it was, came on deck. The Admiral ordered him and others to launch the boat, which was on the poop, and lay out an anchor astern. The master, with several others, got into the boat, and the Admiral thought that they did so with the object of obeying his orders. But they did so in order to take refuge with the caravel, which was half a league to leeward. The caravel would not allow them to come on board, acting judiciously, and they therefore returned to the ship; but the caravel's boat arrived first. When the Admiral saw that his own people fled in this way, the water rising and the ship being across the sea, seeing no other course, he ordered the masts to be cut away and the ship to be lightened as much as possible, to see if she would come off. But, as the water continued to rise, nothing more could be done. Her side fell over across the sea, but it was nearly calm. Then the timbers opened, and the ship was lost. The Admiral went to the caravel to arrange about the reception of the ship's crew, and as a light breeze was blowing from the land, and continued during the greater part of the night, while it was unknown how far the bank extended, he hove her to until daylight. He then went back to the ship, inside the reef; first having sent a boat on shore with Diego de Arana of Cordova, Alguazil of the Fleet, and Pedro Gutierrez, gentleman of the King's bedchamber, to inform the king, who had invited the ships to come on the previous Saturday. His town was about a league and a half from the sand-bank. They reported that he wept when he heard the news, and he sent all his people with large canoes to unload the ship. This was done, and they landed all there was between decks in a very short time. Such was the great promptitude and diligence shown by that king. He himself, with brothers and relations, was actively assisting as well in the ship as in the care of the property when it was landed, that all might be properly guarded. Now and then he sent one of his relations weeping to the Admiral, to console him, saying that he must not feel sorrow or annoyance, for he would supply all that was needed. The Admiral assured the Sovereigns that there could not have been such good watch kept in any part of Castille, for that there was not even a needle missing. He ordered that all the property should be placed by some houses which the king placed at his disposal, until they were emptied, when everything would be stowed and guarded in them. Armed men were placed round the stores to watch all night. "The king and all his people wept. They are a loving people, without covetousness, and fit for anything; and I assure your Highnesses that there is no better land nor people. They love their neighbours as themselves, and their speech is the sweetest and gentlest in the world, and always with a smile. Men and women go as naked as when their mothers bore them. Your Highnesses should believe that they have very good customs among themselves. The king is a man of remarkable presence, and with a certain self-contained manner that is a pleasure to see. They have good memories, wish to see everything, and ask the use of what they see." All this is written by the Admiral.

Wednesday, 26th of December.

To-day, at sunrise, the king of that land came to the caravel *Niña*, where the Admiral was, and said to him, almost weeping, that he need not be sorry,

for that he would give him all he had; that he had
placed two large houses at the disposal of the Christians
who were on shore, and that he would give more
if they were required, and as many canoes as could
load from the ship and discharge on shore, with as
many people as were wanted. This had all been done
yesterday, without so much as a needle being missed.
"So honest are they," says the Admiral, "without any
covetousness for the goods of others, and so above all
was that virtuous king." While the Admiral was
talking to him, another canoe arrived from a different
place, bringing some pieces of gold, which the people
in the canoe wanted to exchange for a hawk's bell;
for there was nothing they desired more than these
bells. They had scarcely come alongside when they
called and held up the gold, saying *Chuq chuq* for the
bells, for they are quite mad about them. After the
king had seen this, and when the canoes which came
from other places had departed, he called the Admiral
and asked him to give orders that one of the bells was
to be kept for another day, when he would bring four
pieces of gold the size of a man's hand. The Admiral
rejoiced to hear this, and afterwards a sailor, who came
from the shore, told him that it was wonderful what
pieces of gold the men on shore were getting in exchange
for next to nothing. For a needle they got a piece of
gold worth two *castellanos*, and that this was nothing
to what it would be within a month. The king re·
joiced much when he saw that the Admiral was pleased.
He understood that his friend wanted much gold, and
he said, by signs, that he knew where there was, in
the vicinity, a very large quantity; so that he must
be in good heart, for he should have as much as he

wanted. He gave some account of it, especially saying
that in *Cipango*, which they call *Cibao*, it is so abundant
that it is of no value, and that they will bring it,
although there is also much more in the island of
Española, which they call *Bohio*, and in the province
of *Caritaba*. The king dined on board the caravel
with the Admiral and afterwards went on shore, where
he received the Admiral with much honour. He gave
him a collation consisting of three or four kinds of
yams, with shellfish and game, and other viands they
have, besides the bread they call *cazavi*. He then took
the Admiral to see some groves of trees near the houses,
and they were accompanied by at least a thousand
people, all naked. The Lord had on a shirt and a pair
of gloves, given to him by the Admiral, and he was
more delighted with the gloves than with anything
else. In his manner of eating, both as regards the
high-bred air and the peculiar cleanliness, he clearly
showed his nobility. After he had eaten, he remained
some time at table, and they brought him certain herbs,
with which he rubbed his hands. The Admiral thought
that this was done to make them soft, and they also
gave him water for his hands. After the meal he took
the Admiral to the beach. The Admiral then sent
for a Turkish bow and a quiver of arrows, and took
a shot at a man of his company, who had been warned.
The chief, who knew nothing about arms, as they
neither have them nor use them, thought this a wonderful thing. He, however, began to talk of those of
Caniba, whom they call *Caribes*. They come to capture the natives, and have bows and arrows without
iron, of which there is no memory in any of these lands,
nor of steel, nor any other metal except gold and

copper. Of copper the Admiral had only seen very
little. The Admiral said, by signs, that the Sovereigns
of Castille would order the Caribs to be destroyed, and
that all should be taken with their heads tied together.
He ordered a lombard and a hand-gun to be fired off,
and seeing the effect caused by its force and what the
shots penetrated, the king was astonished. When his
people heard the explosion they all fell on the ground.
They brought the Admiral a large mask, which had
pieces of gold for the eyes and ears and in other parts,
and this they gave, with other trinkets of gold that
the same king had put on the head and round the neck
of the Admiral, and of other Christians, to whom they
also gave many pieces. The Admiral received much
pleasure and consolation from these things, which
tempered the anxiety and sorrow he felt at the loss
of the ship. He knew our Lord had caused the ship
to stop here, that a settlement might be formed.
"From this," he says, "originated so many things
that, in truth, the disaster was really a piece of good
fortune. For it is certain that, if I had not lost the
ship, I should have gone on without anchoring in this
place, which is within a great bay, having two or three
reefs of rock. I should not have left people in the
country during this voyage, nor even, if I had desired
to leave them, should I have been able to obtain so
much information, nor such supplies and provisions
for a fortress. And true it is that many people had
asked me to give them leave to remain. Now I have
given orders for a tower and a fort, both well built,
and a large cellar, not because I believe that such
defences will be necessary. I believe that with the
force I have with me I could subjugate the whole

ısland, which I believe to be larger than Portugal, and the population double. But they are naked and without arms, and hopelessly timid. Still, it is advisable to build this tower, being so far from your Highnesses. The people may thus know the skill of the subjects of your Highnesses, and what they can do; and will obey them with love and fear. So they make preparations to build the fortress, with provision of bread and wine for more than a year, with seeds for sowing, the ship's boat, a caulker and carpenter, a gunner and cooper. Many among these men have a great desire to serve your Highnesses and to please me, by finding out where the mine is whence the gold is brought. Thus everything is got in readiness to begin the work. Above all, it was so calm that there was scarcely wind nor wave when the ship ran aground."

[Columbus, now in the *Niña*, weighed anchor on January 4, and sailed a short distance to the east to the neighbourhood of Monte Cristi. Here he was joined by the *Pinta*, and the captain Martin Pinzon excused himself for his absence of more than six weeks, "saying that he had parted company against his will, giving reasons for it. But the Admiral says that they were all false; and that on the night when Pinzon parted company he was influenced by pride and covetousness[1]."

They continued coasting to the east as far as Samana Bay, where they met with Indians armed with bows and arrows, who attacked them. Columbus however succeeded in making peace with their chief.

From this bay on January 16 they started for Spain.

[1] It is now thought that Columbus was very unjust to Pinzon, and that to him was due a large share of credit for the success of the expedition.

The voyage was peaceful until the middle of February, when a furious hurricane overtook them and separated the two vessels. Columbus, fearing that he might never return with his great news, wrote an account of his discoveries on parchment, rolled it up in waxed cloth, and put it inside a wooden barrel, which was thrown into the sea.

Both vessels however weathered the storm; the *Pinta* reaching a port in Galicia, and the *Niña*, after touching at the Azores, coming to anchor in the Tagus on March 4. Thence Columbus, after visiting the King and Queen of Portugal, sailed on March 13, and reached his starting-point at Palos on the 15th.]

COLUMBUS. SECOND VOYAGE
(1493–1496)

A Letter addressed to the Chapter of Seville by Dr Chanca, native of that city, and physician to the fleet of Columbus, in his second voyage to the West Indies, describing the principal events which occurred during that voyage.

Most noble sir,—Since the occurrences which I relate in private letters to other persons, are not of such general interest as those which are contained in this epistle, I have resolved to give you a distinct narrative of the events of our voyage, as well as to treat of the other matters which form the subject of my petition to you. The news I have to communicate is as follows : The expedition which their Catholic Majesties sent, by Divine permission, from Spain to the Indies, under the command of Christopher Columbus, Admiral of the ocean, left Cadiz on the twenty-fifth of September, of the year 1493, with wind and weather favourable for the voyage. This wind lasted two days, during which time we managed to make fifty leagues ; the weather then changing, we made little or no progress for the next two days ; it pleased God, however, after this, to restore us fine weather, so that in two days more we reached the Great Canary. Here we put into harbour, which we were obliged to do, to repair one of

the ships which made a great deal of water; we remained all that day, and on the following set sail again,
but were several times becalmed, so that we were four
or five days before we reached Gomera. We had to
remain at Gomera one day to lay in our stores of meat,
wood, and as much water as we could stow, preparatory
to the long voyage which we expected to make without
seeing land: thus through the delay at these two ports,
and being fixed in a calm one day after leaving Gomera,
we were nineteen or twenty days before we arrived
at the Island of Ferro. After this we had, by the goodness of God, a return of fine weather, more continuous
than any fleet ever enjoyed during so long a voyage;
so that leaving Ferro on the thirteenth of October,
within twenty days we came in sight of land: and we
should have seen it in fourteen or fifteen days, if the
ship *Capitana* had been as good a sailer as the other
vessels; for many times the others had to shorten sail,
because they were leaving us much behind. During
all this time we had great good fortune, for throughout
the voyage we encountered no storm, with the exception of one on St Simon's eve, which for four hours put
us in considerable jeopardy.

On the first Sunday after All Saints, namely the
third of November, about dawn, a pilot of the ship
Capitana cried out: "The reward, I see the land!"

The joy of the people was so great, that it was
wonderful to hear their cries and exclamations of
pleasure; and they had good reason to be delighted;
for they had become so wearied of bad living, and of
working the water out of the ships, that all sighed
most anxiously for land. The pilots of the fleet
reckoned on that day, that between leaving Ferro

and first reaching land, we had made eight hundred leagues; others said seven hundred and eighty (so that the difference was not great), and three hundred more between Ferro and Cadiz, making in all eleven hundred leagues; I do not therefore feel as one who had not seen enough of the water. On the morning of the aforesaid Sunday, we saw lying before us an island, and soon on the right hand another appeared: the first was high and mountainous on the side nearest to us; the other flat, and very thickly wooded: as soon as it became lighter, other islands began to appear on both sides; so that on that day, there were six islands to be seen lying in different directions, and most of them of considerable size. We directed our course towards that which we had first seen, and reaching the coast, we proceeded more than a league in search of a port where we might anchor, but without finding one: all that part of the island which we could observe, appeared mountainous, very beautiful, and green even up to the water, which was delightful to see, for at that season, there is scarcely any thing green in our own country. When we found that there was no harbour there, the Admiral decided that we should go to the other island, which appeared on the right, and which was at four or five leagues distance: one vessel however still remained on the first island all that day seeking for a harbour, in case it should be necessary to return thither. At length, having found a good one, where they saw both people and dwellings, they returned that night to the fleet, which had put into harbour at the other island, and there the Admiral, accompanied by a great number of men, landed with the royal banner in his hands, and took formal

possession on behalf of their Majesties. This island was
filled with an astonishingly thick growth of wood; the
variety of unknown trees, some bearing fruit and some
flowers, was surprising, and indeed every spot was
covered with verdure. We found there a tree whose
leaf had the finest smell of cloves that I have ever met
with; it was like a laurel leaf, but not so large: but
I think it was a species of laurel. There were wild
fruits of various kinds, some of which our men, not
very prudently, tasted; and upon only touching them
with their tongues, their countenances became inflamed,
and such great heat and pain followed, that they seemed
to be mad, and were obliged to resort to refrigerants
to cure themselves. We found no signs of any people
in this island, and concluded it was uninhabited; we
remained only two hours, for it was very late when
we landed, and on the following morning we left for
another very large island, situated below this at the
distance of seven or eight leagues. We approached
it under the side of a great mountain, that seemed
almost to reach the skies, in the middle of which rose
a peak, higher than all the rest of the mountain, whence
many streams diverged into different channels, especially
towards the part at which we arrived. At three leagues
distance, we could see an immense fall of water, which
discharged itself from such a height that it appeared
to fall from the sky; it was seen from so great a distance that it occasioned many wagers to be laid on
board the ships, some maintaining that it was but a
series of white rocks, and others that it was water.
When we came nearer to it, it showed itself distinctly,
and it was the most beautiful thing in the world to see
from how great a height and from what a small space

The earliest picture of Indians

so large a fall of water was discharged.   As soon as
we neared the island the Admiral ordered a light caravel
to run along the coast to search for a harbour; the
captain put into land in a boat, and seeing some houses,
leapt on shore and went up to them, the inhabitants
fleeing at sight of our men; he then went into the
houses and there found various household articles that
had been left unremoved, from which he took two
parrots, very large and quite different from any we
had before seen.   He found a great quantity of cotton,
both spun and prepared for spinning, and articles of
food, of all of which he brought away a portion; besides
these, he also brought away four or five bones of human
arms and legs.   On seeing these we suspected that we
were amongst the Caribbee islands, which are inhabited
by cannibals; for the Admiral, guided by the information respecting their situation which he had received
from the Indians of the islands discovered in his former
voyage, had directed his course with a view to their
discovery, both because they were the nearest to Spain,
and because this was the direct track for the island of
Española, where he had left some of his people.   Thither,
by the goodness of God and the wise management of
the Admiral, we came in as straight a track as if we
had sailed by a well-known and frequented route.   This
island is very large, and on the side where we arrived
it seemed to us to be twenty-five leagues in length.   We
sailed more than two leagues along the shore in search
of a harbour; on the part towards which we moved
appeared very high mountains, and on that which we
left extensive plains; on the sea coast there were a few
small villages, whose inhabitants fled as soon as they
saw the sails: at length after proceeding two leagues

we found a port late in the evening. That night the
Admiral resolved that some of the men should land
at break of day in order to confer with the natives,
and learn what sort of people they were; although it
was suspected, from the appearance of those who had
fled at our approach, that they were naked, like those
whom the Admiral had seen in his former voyage. In
the morning several detachments under their respective
captains sailed forth; one of them arrived at the dinner
hour, and brought away a boy of about fourteen years
of age, as it afterwards appeared, who said that he was
one of the prisoners taken by these people. The others
divided themselves, and one party took a little boy
whom a man was leading by the hand, but who left
him and fled; this boy they sent on board immediately
with some of our men; others remained, and took certain women, natives of the island, together with other
women from among the captives who came of their
own accord. One captain of this last company, not
knowing that any intelligence of the people had been
obtained, advanced farther into the island and lost
himself, with the six men who accompanied him: they
could not find their way back until after four days,
when they lighted upon the sea shore, and following
the line of coast returned to the fleet. We had
already looked upon them as killed and eaten by the
people that are called Caribbees; for we could not account for their long absence in any other way, since
they had among them some pilots who by their knowledge of the stars could navigate either to or from Spain,
so that we imagined that they could not lose themselves
in so small a space. On this first day of our landing
several men and women came on the beach up to the

water's edge, and gazed at the ships in astonishment at so novel a sight; and when a boat pushed on shore in order to speak with them, they cried out, "tayno, tayno," which is as much as to say, "good, good," and waited for the landing of the sailors, standing by the boat in such a manner that they might escape when they pleased. The result was, that none of the men could be persuaded to join us, and only two were taken by force, who were secured and led away. More than twenty of the female captives were taken with their own consent, and other women natives of the island were surprised and carried off: several of the boys, who were captives, came to us fleeing from the natives of the island who had taken them prisoners. We remained eight days in this port in consequence of the loss of the aforesaid captain, and went many times on shore, passing amongst the dwellings and villages which were on the coast; we found a vast number of human bones and skulls hung up about the houses, like vessels intended for holding various things. There were very few men to be seen here, and the women informed us that this was in consequence of ten canoes having gone to make an attack upon other islands. These islanders appeared to us to be more civilized than those that we had hitherto seen; for although all the Indians have houses of straw, yet the houses of these people are constructed in a much superior fashion, are better stocked with provisions, and exhibit more evidences of industry, both on the part of the men and the women. They had a considerable quantity of cotton, both spun and prepared for spinning, and many cotton sheets, so well woven as to be no way inferior to those of our country. We enquired of the women, who were prisoners in the island, what people these islanders were: they replied that they were Caribbees. As soon as they learned that we abhorred such people, on account of their evil practice of eating human flesh, they were much delighted; and, after that, if they brought forward any woman or man of the Caribbees, they informed us (but secretly), that they were such, still evincing by their dread of their conquerors, that they belonged to a vanquished nation, though they knew them all to be in our power.

We were enabled to distinguish which of the women were natives, and which were captives, by the Caribbees wearing on each leg two bands of woven cotton, the one fastened round the knee, and the other round the ankle; by this means they make the calves of their legs large, and the above-mentioned parts very small, which I imagine that they regard as a matter of refinement: by this peculiarity we distinguished them. The habits of these Caribbees are brutal. There are three islands: the one called Turuqueira; the other, which was the first that we saw, is called Ceyre; the third is called Ayay: there is a resemblance amongst all these, as if they were of one race, and they do no injury to each other; but each and all of them wage war against the other neighbouring islands, and for the purpose of attacking them, make voyages of a hundred and fifty leagues at sea, with their numerous canoes, which are a small kind of craft with one mast. Their arms are arrows, in the place of iron weapons, and as they have no iron, some of them point their arrows with tortoise-shell, and others make their arrow heads of fish spines, which are naturally barbed like coarse saws: these prove dangerous weapons to a naked people like the Indians, and may inflict severe injury, but to men of our nation, are not very formidable.   In their attacks upon the neighbouring islands, these people take as many of the women as they can, especially those who are young and beautiful, and keep them.   Such of their male enemies as they can take alive, they bring to their houses to make a feast of them, and those who are dead they devour at once.   They say that man's flesh is so good, that there is nothing like it in the world ; and this is pretty evident, for of the bones which we found in their houses, they had gnawed everything that could be gnawed, so that nothing remained of them, but what from its great hardness could not be eaten : in one of the houses we found the neck of a man, undergoing the process of cooking.

At the end of four days arrived the captain who had lost himself with his companions, of whose return we had by this time given up all hope ; for other parties had been twice sent out to seek him, one of which came back on the same day that he rejoined us, without having gained any information respecting the wanderers ; we rejoiced at their arrival, regarding it as a new accession to our numbers.   The captain and the men who accompanied him brought back some women and boys, ten in number : neither this party, nor those who went out to seek them, had seen any of the men of the island, which must have arisen either from their having fled, or possibly from there being but very few men in that locality ; for, as the women informed us, ten canoes had gone away to make an attack upon the neighbouring islands.   The wanderers had returned from the mountains in such an emaciated condition, that it was distressing to see them ; when we asked them how

it was that they lost themselves, they said that the
trees were so thick and close that they could not see
the sky; some of them who were mariners had climbed
the trees to get a sight of the stars, but could never
see them, and if they had not found their way to the
sea coast, it would have been impossible to have returned to the fleet. We left this island eight days
after our arrival. The next day at noon we saw another
island, not very large, at about twelve leagues distance
from the one we were leaving; the greater part of the
first day of our departure we were kept close in to the
coast of this island by a calm, but as the Indian women,
whom we brought with us, said that it was not inhabited,
but had been dispeopled by the Caribbees, we made no
stay in it. On that evening we saw another island:
and in the night finding there were some sandbanks
near, we dropped anchor, not venturing to proceed
until the morning. On the morrow another island
appeared, of considerable size, but we touched at none
of these because we were anxious to convey consolation
to our people who had been left in Española; but it
did not please God to grant us our desire, as will hereafter appear. Another day at the dinner hour we
arrived at an island which seemed to be worth finding,
for judging by the extent of cultivation in it, it appeared
very populous. We went thither and put into harbour,
when the Admiral immediately sent on shore a well
manned barge to hold speech with the Indians, in order
to ascertain what race they were, and also because we
considered it necessary to gain some information respecting our course; although it afterwards plainly
appeared that the Admiral, who had never made that
passage before, had taken a very correct route. But

since doubtful questions ought always by investigation
to be reduced as nearly to a certainty as possible, he
wished that communication should be held with the
natives at once, and some of the men who went in the
barge leapt on shore and went up to a village, whence
the inhabitants had already withdrawn and hidden
themselves. They took in this island five or six women
and some boys, most of whom were captives, like those
in the other island; we learned from the women whom
we had brought with us, that the natives of this place
also were Caribbees. As this barge was about to return
to the ships with the capture which they had taken,
a canoe came along the coast containing four men, two
women, and a boy; and when they saw the fleet they
were so stupefied with amazement, that for a good hour
they remained motionless at the distance of nearly
two gunshots from the ships. In this position they
were seen by those who were in the barge and also by
all the fleet. Meanwhile those in the barge moved
towards the canoe, but so close in shore, that the
Indians, in their perplexity and astonishment as to
what all this could mean, never saw them, until they
were so near that escape was impossible; for our men
pressed on them so rapidly that they could not get
away, although they made considerable effort to do so.

When the Caribbees saw that all attempt at flight
was useless, they most courageously took to their bows,
both women and men; I say most courageously, because they were only four men and two women, and our
people were twenty-five in number. Two of our men
were wounded by the Indians, one with two arrow-
shots in his breast, and another with one in his side, and
if it had not happened that they carried shields and

wooden bucklers, and that they got near them with the
barge and upset their canoe, most of them would have
been killed with their arrows. After their canoe was
upset, they remained in the water swimming and occa-
sionally wading (for there were shallows in that part),
still using their bows as much as they could, so that
our men had enough to do to take them : and after all
there was one of them, whom they were unable to secure,
till he had received a mortal wound with a lance, and
whom thus wounded they took to the ships. The
difference between these Caribbees and the other
Indians, with respect to dress, consists in their wearing
their hair very long, while the others have it clipt
irregularly and paint their heads with crosses and a
hundred thousand different devices, each according to
his fancy; which they do with sharpened reeds. All
of them, both the Caribbees and the others, are beardless, so that it is a rare thing to find a man with a beard :
the Caribbees whom we took had their eyes and eyebrows stained, which I imagine they do from ostenta-
tion and to give them a more formidable appearance.
One of these captives said, that in an island belonging
to them called Ceyre (which is the first we saw, though
we did not go to it), there is a great quantity of gold ;
and that if we were to take them nails and tools with
which to make their canoes, we might bring away as
much gold as we liked. On the same day we left that
island, having been there no more than six or seven
hours ; and steering for another point of land which
appeared to lie in our intended course, we reached it
by night. On the morning of the following day we
coasted along it, and found it to be a large extent of
country, but not continuous, for it was divided into

more than forty islets. The land was very high and
most of it barren, an appearance which we have never
observed in any of the islands visited by us before or
since: the surface of the ground seemed to suggest
the probability of its containing metals. None of us
went on shore here, but a small lateen caravel went
up to one of the islets and found in it some fishermen's
huts; the Indian women whom we brought with us
said they were not inhabited. We proceeded along
the coast the greater part of that day, and on the
evening of the next we discovered another island
called Burenquen, which we judged to be thirty leagues
in length, for we were coasting along it the whole of
one day. This island is very beautiful and apparently
fertile: hither the Caribbees come with the view of
subduing the inhabitants, and often carry away many
of the people. These islanders have no boats nor
any knowledge of navigation; but, as our captives
inform us, they use bows as well as the Caribbees, and
if by chance, when they are attacked, they succeed in
taking any of their invaders, they will eat them in like
manner as the Caribbees themselves, in the contrary
event, would devour them. We remained two days
in this island, and a great number of our men went on
shore, but could never get speech of the natives, who
had all fled, from fear of the Caribbees. All the above-
mentioned islands were discovered in this voyage, the
Admiral having seen nothing of them in his former
voyage; they are all very beautiful and possess a
most luxuriant soil, but this last island appeared to
exceed all the others in beauty. Here terminated the
islands, which on the side towards Spain had not been
seen before by the Admiral, although we regard it as

a matter of certainty that there is land more than
forty leagues beyond the foremost of these newly discovered islands, on the side nearest to Spain. We
believe this to be the case, because two days before we
saw land we observed some birds called rabihorcados (or
pelicans, marine birds of prey which do not sit or sleep
upon the water), making circumvolutions in the air at
the close of evening previous to taking their flight
towards land for the night. These birds could not be
going to settle at more than twelve or fifteen leagues
distance, because it was late in the evening, and this
was on our right hand on the side towards Spain; from
which we all judged that there was land there still un-
discovered; but we did not go in search of it, because
it would have taken us round out of our intended route.
I hope that in a few voyages it will be discovered. It
was at dawn that we left the before-mentioned island
of Burenquen, and on that day before nightfall we
caught sight of land, which though not recognized by
any of those who had come hither in the former voyage,
we believed to be Española, from the information given
us by the Indian women whom we had with us: and
in this island we remain at present. Between Española
and Burenquen another island appeared at a distance,
but of no great size. When we reached Española, the
land, at the part where we approached it, was low and
very flat, on seeing which, a general doubt arose as to
its identity; for, neither the Admiral nor his companions, on the previous voyage, had seen it on this
side.

The island being large, is divided into provinces;
the part which we first touched at, is called Hayti;
another province adjoining it, they call Xamaná; and

the next province is named Bohio, where we now are.
These provinces are again subdivided, for they are of
great extent. Those who have seen the length of its
coast, state that it is two hundred leagues long, and I
myself should judge it not to be less than a hundred
and fifty leagues: as to its breadth, nothing is hitherto
known; it is now forty days since a caravel left
us with the view of circumnavigating it, and is not
yet returned. The country is very remarkable, and
contains a vast number of large rivers, and extensive
chains of mountains, with broad open valleys, and
the mountains are very high: it does not appear that
the grass is ever cut throughout the year. I do not
think they have any winter in this part, for near
Navidad (at Christmas) were found many birds-nests,
some containing the young birds, and others containing eggs. No four-footed animal has ever been seen
in this or any of the other islands, except some dogs
of various colours, as in our own country, but in shape
like large house-dogs; and also some little animals, in
colour, size, and fur, like a rabbit, with long tails,
and feet like those of a rat; these animals climb up
the trees, and many who have tasted them, say they
are very good to eat: there are not any wild beasts.
There are great numbers of small snakes, and some
lizards, but not many; for the Indians consider them
as great a luxury as we do pheasants: they are of the
same size as ours, but different in shape. In a small
adjacent island (close by a harbour called Monte
Cristi, where we stayed several days), our men saw
an enormous kind of lizard, which they said was as
large round as a calf, with a tail as long as a lance,
which they often went out to kill: but bulky as it was,

it got into the sea, so that they could not catch it.
There are, both in this and the other islands, an infinite
number of birds like those in our own country, and
many others such as we had never seen. No kind of
domestic fowl has been seen here, with the exception
of some ducks in the houses in Zuruquia; these ducks
were larger than those of Spain, though smaller than
geese,—very pretty, with tufts on their heads, most of
them as white as snow, but some black.

We ran along the coast of this island nearly a hundred leagues, concluding that within this range we
should find the spot where the Admiral had left some
of his men, and which we supposed to be about the
middle of the coast. As we passed by the province
called Xamaná, we sent on shore one of the Indians,
who had been taken in the previous voyage, clothed,
and carrying some trifles, which the Admiral had
ordered to be given him. On that day died one of our
sailors, a Biscayan, who had been wounded in the
affray with the Caribbees, when they were captured,
as I have already described, through their want of
caution. As we were proceeding along the coast, an
opportunity was afforded for a boat to go on shore to
bury him, the boat being accompanied by two caravels
to protect it. When they reached the shore, a great
number of Indians came out to the boat, some of them
wearing necklaces and ear-rings of gold, and expressed a
wish to accompany the Spaniards to the ships; but our
men refused to take them, because they had not received
permission from the Admiral. When the Indians
found that they would not take them, two of them got
into a small canoe, and went up to one of the caravels
that had put in to shore; they were received on board

with great kindness, and taken to the Admiral's ship, where, through the medium of an interpreter, they related that a certain king had sent them to ascertain who we were, and to invite us to land, adding that they had plenty of gold, and also of provisions, to which we should be welcome. The Admiral desired that shirts, and caps, and other trifles, should be given to each of them, and said that as he was going to the place where Guacamari dwelt, he would not stop then, but that on a future day he should have the opportunity of seeing him, and with that they departed. We continued our route till we came to an harbour called Monte Cristi, where we remained two days, in order to observe the position of the land; for the Admiral had an objection to the spot, where his men had been left with the view of forming a station. We went on shore therefore to survey the formation of the land: there was a large river of excellent water close by; but the ground was inundated, and very ill-calculated for habitation. As we went on making our observations on the river and the land, some of our men found two dead bodies by the river's side, one with a rope round his neck, and the other with one round his foot: this was on the first day of our landing. On the following day they found two other corpses farther on, and one of these was observed to have a great quantity of beard; this was regarded as a very suspicious circumstance by many of our people, because, as I have already said, all the Indians are beardless. This harbour is twelve leagues from the place where the Spaniards had been left under the protection of Guacamari, the king of that province, whom I suppose to be one of the chief men of the island. After two days we set sail for that spot, but as it was late when we arrived there, and there were some shoals, where the Admiral's ship had been lost, we did not venture to put in close to the shore, but remained that night at a little less than a league from the coast, waiting until the morning, when we might enter securely. On that evening, a canoe, containing five or six Indians, came out at a considerable distance from where we were, and approached us with great celerity. The Admiral believing that he insured our safety by keeping the sails set, would not wait for them; they, however, perseveringly rowed up to us within gunshot, and then stopped to look at us; but when they saw that we did not wait for them, they put back and went away. After we had anchored that night at the spot in question, the Admiral ordered two guns to be fired, to see if the Spaniards, who had remained with Guacamari, would fire in return, for they also had guns with them; but when we received no reply, and could not perceive any fires, nor the slightest symptom of habitations on the spot, the spirits of our people became much depressed, and they began to entertain the suspicion which the circumstances were naturally calculated to excite. While all were in this desponding mood, and when four or five hours of the night had passed away, the same canoe which we had seen in the evening, came up, and the Indians with a loud voice addressed the captain of the caravel, which they first approached, inquiring for the Admiral; they were conducted to the Admiral's vessel, but would not go on board till he had spoken to them, and they had asked for a light, in order to assure themselves that it was he who conversed with them. One of them was a cousin of Guacamari, who had been sent by him once

before: it appeared, that after they had turned back
the previous evening, they had been charged by Guacamari with two masks of gold as a present; one for
the Admiral, the other for a captain who had accompanied him on the former voyage. They remained
on board for three hours, talking with the Admiral in
the presence of all of us, he showing much pleasure in
their conversation, and inquiring respecting the welfare
of the Spaniards whom he had left behind. Guacamari's cousin replied, that those who remained were
all well, but that some of them had died of disease, and
others had been killed in quarrels that had arisen
amongst them: he said also that the province had
been invaded, by two kings named Caonabó and Mayreni, who had burned the habitations of the people;
and that Guacamari was at some distance, lying ill of
a wound in his leg, which was the occasion of his not
appearing, but that he would come on the next day.
The Indians then departed, saying they would return
on the following day with the said Guacamari, and left
us consoled for that night. On the morning of the
next day, we were expecting that Guacamari would
come; and, in the meantime, some of our men landed
by command of the Admiral, and went to the spot
where the Spaniards had formerly been: they found
the building which they had inhabited, and which they
had in some degree fortified with a palisade, burnt
and levelled with the ground; they found also some
rags and stuffs which the Indians had brought to throw
upon the house. They observed too that the Indians
who were seen near the spot, looked very shy, and
dared not approach, but, on the contrary, fled from
them. This appeared strange to us, for the Admiral

had told us that in the former voyage, when he arrived
at this place, so many came in canoes to see us, that
there was no keeping them off; and as we now saw
that they were suspicious of us, it gave us a very un-
favourable impression. We threw trifles, such as
buttons and beads, towards them, in order to conciliate them, but only four, a relation of Guacamari's
and three others, took courage to enter the boat, and
were rowed on board. When they were asked concerning the Spaniards, they replied that all of them
were dead: we had been told this already by one of
the Indians whom we had brought from Spain, and
who had conversed with the two Indians that on the
former occasion came on board with their canoe, but
we had not believed it. Guacamari's kinsman was
asked who had killed them: he replied that king
Caonabó and king Mayreni had made an attack upon
them, and burnt the buildings on the spot, that many
were wounded in the affray, and among them Guacamari, who had received a wound in his thigh, and had
retired to some distance: he also stated that he wished
to go and fetch him; upon which some trifles were
given to him, and he took his departure for the place
of Guacamari's abode. All that day we remained in
expectation of them, and when we saw that they did
not come, many suspected that the Indians who had
been on board the night before had been drowned; for
they had had wine given them two or three times, and
they had come in a small canoe that might be easily
upset. The next morning the Admiral went on shore,
taking some of us with him; we went to the spot where
the settlement had been, and found it utterly destroyed
by fire, and the clothes of the Spaniards lying about

upon the grass, but on that occasion we saw no dead body.   There were many different opinions amongst us ; some suspecting that Guacamari himself was concerned in the betrayal and death of the Christians ; others thought not, because his own residence was burnt : so that it remained a very doubtful question.   The Admiral ordered all the ground which had been occu-pied by the fortifications of the Spaniards to be searched, for he had left orders with them to bury all the gold that they might get.   While this was being done, the Admiral wished to examine a spot at about a league's distance, which seemed to be suitable for building a town, for there was yet time to do so ;—and some of us went thither with him, making our observations of the land as we went along the coast, until we reached a village of seven or eight houses, which the Indians forsook when they saw us approach, carrying away what they could, and leaving the things which they could not remove, hidden amongst the grass, around the houses.   These people are so degraded that they have not even the sense to select a fitting place to live in ; those who dwell on the shore, build for themselves the most miserable hovels that can be imagined, and all the houses are so covered with grass and dampness, that I wonder how they can contrive to exist.   In these houses we found many things belonging to the Spaniards, which it could not be supposed they would have bartered ; such as a very handsome Moorish mantle, which had not been unfolded since it was brought from Spain, stockings and pieces of cloth, also an anchor belonging to the ship which the Admiral had lost here on the previous voyage ; with other articles, which the more confirmed our suspicions.   On

examining some things which had been very cautiously
sewn up in a small basket, we found a man's head
wrapped up with great care; this we judged might be
the head of a father, or mother, or of some person whom
they much regarded: I have since heard that many
were found in the same state, which makes me believe
that our first impression was the true one. After this
we returned. We went on the same day to the site of
the settlement; and when we arrived, we found many
Indians, who had regained their courage, bartering
gold with our men: they had bartered to the extent
of a mark: we also learned that they had shown where
the bodies of eleven of the dead Spaniards were laid,
which were already covered with the grass that had
grown over them; and they all with one voice asserted
that Caonabó and Mayreni had killed them; but notwithstanding all this, we began to hear complaints that
one of the Spaniards had taken three women to himself,
and another four; from whence we drew the inference
that jealousy was the cause of the misfortune that had
occurred. On the next morning, as no spot in that
vicinity appeared suitable for our making a settlement,
the Admiral ordered a caravel to go in one direction to
look for a convenient locality, while some of us went
with him another way. In the course of our explora-
tions, we discovered a harbour, of great security; the
neighbourhood of which, so far as regarded the formation of the land, was excellent for habitation; but as
it was far from any mine of gold, the neighbourhood
of which was very desirable, the Admiral decided that
we should settle in some spot which would give us
greater certainty of attaining that object, provided
the position of the land should prove equally convenient.

On our return, we found the other caravel arrived, in
which Melchior and four or five other trustworthy
men had been exploring with a similar object.   They
reported that as they went along the coast, a canoe
came out to them in which were two Indians, one of
whom was the brother of Guacamari, and was recognized by a pilot who was in the caravel.   When he
questioned them as to their purpose, they replied that
Guacamari sent to beg the Spaniards to come on shore,
as he was residing near, with as many as fifty families
around him.   The chief men of the party then went on
shore in the boat, proceeded to the place where Guacamari was, and found him stretched on his bed, com-
plaining of a severe wound.   They conferred with him,
and inquired respecting the Spaniards ; his reply was,
in accordance with the account already given by the
others, viz.—that they had been killed by Caonabó
and Mayreni, who also had wounded him in the thigh ;
and in confirmation of his assertion, he showed them
the limb bound up : on seeing which, they concluded
that his statement was correct.   At their departure
he gave to each of them a jewel of gold, according to
his estimation of their respective merits.   The Indians
beat the gold into very thin plates, in order to make
masks of it, and set it in a cement which they make
for that purpose : other ornaments they make of it,
to wear on the head and to hang in the ears and nostrils,
for these also they require it to be thin ; it is not the
massiveness of the gold that they admire in their ornaments, but its showy appearance.   Guacamari desired
them by signs and as well as he was able, to tell the
Admiral that as he was thus wounded, he prayed him to
have the goodness to come to see him.   This adventure

the aforesaid sailors related to the Admiral when he
arrived. The next morning he resolved to go thither,
for the spot could be reached in three hours, being
scarcely three leagues distance from the place where
we were; but as it would be the dinner-hour when we
arrived, we dined before we went on shore. After
dinner, the Admiral gave orders that all the captains
should come with their barges to proceed to the shore,
for already on that morning, previous to our departure,
the aforesaid brother of Guacamari had come to speak
with the Admiral to urge his visit. Then the Admiral
went on shore accompanied by all the principal officers, so
richly dressed that they would have made a distinguished
appearance even in any of our chief cities: he took with
him some articles as presents, having already received
from Guacamari a certain quantity of gold, and it was
reasonable that he should make a commensurate re-
sponse to his acts and expressions of good-will: Guacamari had also provided himself with a present.
When we arrived, we found him stretched upon his
bed, which was made of cotton net-work, and, according to their custom, suspended. He did not arise,
but made from his bed the best gesture of courtesy of
which he was capable. He showed much feeling; with
tears in his eyes lamented the death of the Spaniards,
and began speaking on the subject, explaining to the
best of his power, how some died of disease, others
had gone to Caonabó in search of the mine of gold,
and had there been killed, and that the rest had been
attacked and slain in their own town. According to
the appearance of the dead bodies, it was not two
months since this had happened. Then the Admiral
presented him with eight marks and a half of gold,

six hundred and five pieces of jewellery, of various
colours, and a cap of similar jewel-work, which I think
they ought to value very highly, because in it was a
jewel, for which the Admiral, when presenting it, expressed great veneration.   It appears to me that these
people put more value upon copper than gold.   The
surgeon of the fleet and myself being present, the Admiral told Guacamari that we were skilled in the treat-
ment of human disorders, and wished that he would
shew us his wound; he replied that he was willing;
upon which I said it would be necessary that he should,
if possible, go out of the house, because we could not
see well on account of the place being darkened by the
throng of people; to this he consented, I think more
from timidity than inclination, and left the house
leaning on the arm of the Admiral. After he was seated,
the surgeon approached him and began to untie the
bandage; then he told the Admiral that the wound was
made with a *ciba*, by which he meant with a stone.
When the wound was uncovered, we went up to examine
it: it is certain that there was no more wound on that
leg than on the other, although he cunningly pretended
that it pained him much.   Ignorant as we were of the
facts, it was impossible to come to a definite conclusion.
There were certainly many proofs of an invasion by
a hostile people, so that the Admiral was at a loss what
to do; he with many others thought, however, that
for the present, and until they could ascertain the truth,
they ought to conceal their distrust; for after ascertaining it, they would be able to claim whatever indem-
nity they thought proper.   That evening Guacamari
accompanied the Admiral to the ships, and when they
showed him the horses and other objects of interest,

their novelty struck him with the greatest amazement: he took supper on board, and returned that evening to his house. The Admiral told him that he wished to settle there and to build houses; to which he assented, but said that the place was not wholesome, because it was very damp: and so it most certainly was.

All this passed through the interpretation of two of the Indians who had gone to Spain in the last voyage, who were the sole survivors of seven who had embarked with us; five died on the voyage, and these but narrowly escaped. The next day we anchored in that port: Guacamari sent to know when the Admiral intended leaving, and was told that he should do so on the morrow. The same day Guacamari's brother, and others with him, came on board, bringing gold to barter: on the day of our departure also they bartered a great quantity of gold. There were ten women on board, of those which had been taken in the Caribbee islands, principally from Boriquen, and it was observed that the brother of Guacamari spoke with them; we think that he told them to make an effort to escape that night; for certainly during our first sleep they dropped themselves quietly into the water, and went on shore, so that by the time they were missed they had reached such a distance that only four could be taken by the boats which went in pursuit, and these were secured when just leaving the water: they had to swim considerably more than half a league. The next morning the Admiral sent to desire that Guacamari would cause search to be made for the women who had escaped in the night, and that he would send them back to the ships. When the messengers arrived they found the place forsaken and not 'a soul there;

this strongly confirmed the suspicions of many, but others said they might have removed to another village, as was their custom. That day we remained quiet, because the weather was contrary for our departure. On the next morning the Admiral resolved that as the wind was adverse, it would be well to go with the boats to inspect a port on the coast at two leagues distance further up, to see if the formation of the land was favourable for a settlement; and we went thither with all the ships' boats, leaving the ships in the harbour. As we moved along the coast the people manifested a sense of insecurity, and when we reached the spot to which we were bound all the natives had fled. While we were walking about this place we found an Indian stretched on the hill-side, close by the houses, with a gaping wound in his shoulder caused by a dart, so that he had been disabled from fleeing any further. The natives of this island fight with sharp darts, which they discharge from cross-bows in the same manner as boys in Spain shoot their small arrows, and which they send with considerable skill to a great distance; and certainly upon an unarmed people these weapons are calculated to do serious injury. The wounded man told us that Caonabó and his people had wounded him and burnt the houses of Guacamari. Thus we are still kept in uncertainty respecting the death of our people, on account of the paucity of information on which to form an opinion, and the conflicting and equivocal character of the evidence we have obtained. We did not find the position of the land in this port favourable for healthy habitation, and the Admiral resolved upon returning along the upper coast by which we had come from Spain, because we had had tidings

of gold in that direction. But the weather was so
adverse that it cost more labour to sail thirty leagues
in a backward direction than the whole voyage from
Spain; so that, what with the contrary wind and the
length of the passage, three months had elapsed since
we first set foot on land. It pleased God, however, that
through the check upon our progress caused by contrary winds, we succeeded in finding the best and most
suitable spot that we could have selected for a settlement, where there was an excellent harbour and
abundance of fish, an article of which we stood in
great need from the scarcity of meat. The fish caught
here are very singular and more wholesome than those
of Spain. The climate does not allow the fish to be
kept from one day to another, for all animal food
speedily becomes unwholesome, on account of the
alternate heat and damp.

The land is very rich for all purposes; near the
harbour there are two rivers; one large, and another
of moderate breadth somewhat near to it: the water
is of a very remarkable quality. On the bank of it is
being built a city called Marta, one side of which is
bounded by the water with a ravine of cleft rock, so
that at that part there is no need of fortification; the
other half is girt with a plantation of trees so thick
that a rabbit could scarcely pass through it; and so
green that fire will never be able to burn it. A channel
has been commenced for a branch of the river, which
the managers say they will lead through the middle
of the settlement, and will place on it mills of all kinds
requiring to be worked by water. Great quantities of
vegetables have been planted, which certainly attain
a more luxuriant growth here in eight days than they

would in Spain in twenty.   We were frequently visited
by numbers of Indians, among whom were some of
their caciques or chiefs, and many women.   They all
come loaded with *ages*, a sort of turnip, very excellent
for food, which we dressed in various ways.   This food
was so nutritious as to prove a great support to all of
us after the privations we endured when at sea, which
were more severe than ever were suffered by man; for
as we could not tell what weather it would please God
to send us on our voyage, we were obliged to limit
ourselves most rigorously with regard to food, in order
that, at all events, we might at least have the means
of supporting life : this *age* the Caribbees call *nabi*, and
the Indians *hage*.   The Indians barter gold, provisions,
and everything they bring with them, for tags of laces,
beads, and pins, and pieces of porringers and dishes.
They all, as I have said, go naked as they were born,
except the women of this island, who some of them
wear a covering of cotton, which they bind round their
hips, while others use grass and leaves of trees.   When
they wish to appear full-dressed, both men and women
paint themselves, some black, others white, and various
colours, in so many devices that the effect is very
laughable : they shave some parts of their heads, and
in others wear long tufts of matted hair, which have an
indescribably ridiculous appearance : in short, whatever would be looked upon in our country as character-
istic of a madman, is here regarded by the highest of
the Indians as a mark of distinction.

In our present position, we are in the neighbourhood of many mines of gold, not one of which, we are
told, is more than twenty or twenty-five leagues off:
the Indians say that some of them are in Niti, in the

possession of Caonabó, who killed the Christians; the
others are in another place called Cibao, which, if it
please God, we shall see with our eyes before many
days are over; indeed we should go there at once, but
that we have so many things to provide that we are
not equal to it at present. One third of our people
have fallen sick within the last four or five days, which
I think has principally arisen from the toil and privations of the journey; another cause has been the
variableness of the climate; but I hope in our Lord
that all will be restored to health. My idea of this
people is, that if we could converse with them, they
would all become converted, for they do whatever they
see us do, making genuflections before the altars at
the Ave Maria and the other parts of the devotional
service, and making the sign of the cross. They all
say that they wish to be Christians, although in truth
they are idolaters, for in their houses they have many
kinds of figures: when asked what such a figure was,
they would reply it is a thing of *Turey*, by which they
meant "of Heaven." I made a pretence of throwing
them on the fire, which grieved them so that they began
to weep: they believe that everything we bring comes
from heaven, and therefore call it *Turey*, which, as I
have already said, means heaven in their language.
The first day that I went on shore to sleep, was the
Lord's day: the little time that we have spent on land,
has been so much occupied in seeking for a fitting spot
for the settlement, and in providing necessaries, that
we have had little opportunity of becoming acquainted
with the productions of the soil, yet although the time
has been so short, many marvellous things have been
seen. We have met with trees bearing wool, of a

sufficiently fine quality (according to the opinion of those who are acquainted with the art) to be woven into good cloth; there are so many of these trees that we might load the caravels with wool, although it is troublesome to collect, for the trees are very thorny, but some means may be easily found of overcoming this difficulty. There are also cotton trees as large as peach trees, which produce cotton in the greatest abundance. We found trees producing wax as good both in colour and smell as bees-wax and equally useful for burning, indeed there is no great difference between them. There are vast numbers of trees which yield surprisingly fine turpentine, and a great abundance of tragacanth, also very good. We found other trees which I think bear nutmegs, because the bark tastes and smells like that spice, but at present there is no fruit on them; I saw one root of ginger, which an Indian wore hanging round his neck. There are also aloes; not like those which we have hitherto seen in Spain, but no doubt they are of the same kind as those used by us doctors. A sort of cinnamon also has been found; but, to speak the truth, it is not so fine as that with which we are already acquainted in Spain. I do not know whether this arises from ignorance of the proper season to gather it, or whether the soil does not produce better. We have also seen some yellow myrobalans; at this season they are all lying under the trees, and have a bitter flavour, arising, I think, from the rottenness occasioned by the moisture of the ground; but the taste of such parts as have remained sound, is that of the genuine myrobalan. There is also very good mastic. None of the natives of these islands, as far as we have yet seen, possess any iron; they have,

however, many tools, such as hatchets and axes, made
of stone, which are so handsome and well finished, that
it is wonderful how they contrive to make them without the use of iron. Their food consists of bread,
made of the roots of a vegetable which is between a
tree and a vegetable, and the *age,* which I have already
described as being like the turnip, and very good food;
they use, to season it, a spice called *agi,* which they
also eat with fish, and such birds as they can catch of
the many kinds which abound in the island. They
have, besides, a kind of grain like hazel-nuts, very good
to eat. They eat all the snakes, and lizards, and spiders,
and worms, that they find upon the ground; so that, to
my fancy, their bestiality is greater than that of any
beast upon the face of the earth. The Admiral had at one
time determined to leave the search for the mines until
he had first despatched the ships which were to return
to Spain on account of the great sickness which had
prevailed among the men, but afterwards he resolved
upon sending two bands under the command of two
captains, the one to Cibao, and the other to Niti, where,
as I have already said, Caonabó lived. These parties
went, one of them returning on the twentieth, and the
other on the twenty-first of January. The party that
went to Cibao saw gold in so many places as to seem
almost incredible, for in truth they found it in more than
fifty streamlets and rivers, as well as upon their banks;
so that, the captain said they had only to seek throughout that province, and they would find as much as they
wished. He brought specimens from the different
parts, namely, from the sand of the rivers and small
springs. It is thought, that by digging, it will be found
in greater pieces, for the Indians neither know how

to dig nor have the means of digging more than a hand's depth.   The other captain, who went to Niti, returned also with news of a great quantity of gold in three or four places; of which he likewise brought specimens.

Thus, surely, their Highnesses the King and Queen may henceforth regard themselves as the most prosperous and wealthy Sovereigns in the world; never yet, since the creation, has such a thing been seen or read of; for on the return of the ships from their next voyage, they will be able to carry back such a quantity of gold as will fill with amazement all who hear of it.   Here I think I shall do well to break off my narrative. I think those who do not know me will consider me prolix, and somewhat an exaggerator, but God is my witness, that I have not exceeded, by one tittle, the bounds of truth.

COLUMBUS. THIRD VOYAGE (1498–1500)

The History of a Voyage which Don Christopher
Columbus made the third time that he came to
the Indies, when he discovered terra firma, and
which he sent to their Majesties from the Island
of Hispaniola.

Most serene and most exalted and powerful Princes,
the King and Queen, our Sovereigns. The blessed
Trinity moved your Highnesses to the encouragement
of this enterprise to the Indies; and of its infinite
goodness has made me your messenger therein; as
ambassador for which undertaking I approached your
royal presence, moved by the consideration that I was
appealing to the most exalted monarchs in Christendom,
who exercised so great an influence over the Christian
faith, and its advancement in the world: those who
heard of it looked upon it as impossible, for they fixed
all their hopes on the favours of fortune, and pinned
their faith solely upon chance. I gave to the subject
six or seven years of great anxiety, explaining, to the
best of my ability, how great service might be done
to our Lord, by this undertaking, in promulgating
His sacred name and our holy faith among so many
nations;—an enterprise so exalted in itself, and so
calculated to enhance the glory and immortalize the
renown of the greatest sovereigns. It was also requisite

to refer to the temporal prosperity which was foretold
in the writings of so many trustworthy and wise his-
torians, who related that great riches were to be found
in these parts. And at the same time I thought it
desirable to bring to bear upon the subject, the sayings
and opinions of those who have written upon the
geography of the world. And finally, your Highnesses
came to the determination that the undertaking should
be entered upon. In this your Highnesses exhibited
the noble spirit which has been always manifested by
you on every great subject; for all others who had
thought of the matter or heard it spoken of, unani-
mously treated it with contempt, with the exception
of two friars, who always remained constant in their
belief of its practicability. I, myself, in spite of fatigu-
ing opposition, felt sure that the enterprise would
nevertheless prosper, and continue equally confident
of it to this day, because it is a truth, that though
everything will pass away, the Word of God will not;
and I believe, that every prospect which I hold out
will be accomplished; for it was clearly predicted
concerning these lands, by the mouth of the prophet
Isaiah, in many places in Scripture, that from Spain
the holy name of God was to be spread abroad. Thus
I departed in the name of the Holy Trinity, and returned
very soon, bringing with me an account of the practical
fulfilment of everything I had said. Your Highnesses
again sent me out, and in a short space of time, by
God's mercy, not by   * I discovered three hundred and thirty-three leagues of terra firma on the
eastern side, and seven hundred islands, besides those
which I discovered on the first voyage; I also succeeded

* A gap in the original.

in circumnavigating the island of Española, which is
larger in circumference than all Spain, the inhabitants
of which are countless, and all of whom may be laid
under tribute. It was then that complaints arose,
disparaging the enterprise that I had undertaken,
because, forsooth, I had not immediately sent the ships
home laden with gold,—no allowance being made for
the shortness of the time, and all the other impediments
of which I have already spoken. On this account
(either as a punishment for my sins, or, as I trust, for
my salvation), I was held in detestation, and had
obstacles placed in the way of everything I said or for
which I petitioned. I therefore resolved to apply to
your Highnesses, to inform you of all the wonderful
events that I had experienced, and to explain the reason
of every proposition that I made, making reference
to the nations that I had seen, among whom, and
by whose instrumentality, many souls may be saved.
I related how the natives of Española had been laid
under tribute to your Highnesses, and regarded you
as their sovereigns. And I laid before your Highnesses
abundant samples of gold and copper,—proving the
existence of extensive mines of those metals. I also
laid before your Highnesses many sorts of spices, too
numerous to detail; and I spoke of the great quantity
of brazil-wood, and numberless other articles found
in those lands. All this was of no avail with some
persons; who began, with determined hatred, to speak
ill of the enterprise, not taking into account the service
done to our Lord in the salvation of so many souls,
nor the enhancement of your Highnesses' greatness
to a higher pitch than any earthly prince has yet enjoyed; nor considering, that from the exercise of your

Highnesses' goodness, and the expense incurred, both
spiritual and temporal advantage was to be expected,
and that Spain must in the process of time derive from
thence, beyond all doubt, an unspeakable increase of
wealth.   This might be manifestly seen by the evidences already given in writing in the descriptions of
the voyages already made, which also prove that the
fulfilment of every other hope may be reasonably
expected.   Nor were they affected by the consideration of what great princes throughout the world have
done to increase their fame : as, for example, Solomon,
who sent from Jerusalem, to the uttermost parts of
the east, to see Mount Sopora, in which expedition his
ships were detained three years ; and which mountain
your Highnesses now possess in the island of Española.
Nor, as in the case of Alexander, who sent to observe
the mode of government in the island of Taprobana,
in India ; and Cæsar Nero, to explore the sources of
the Nile, and to learn the causes of its increase in the
summer, when water is needed ; and many other mighty
deeds that princes have done, and which it is allotted to
princes to achieve.   Nor was it of any avail that no
prince of Spain, as far as I have read, has ever hitherto
gained possession of land out of Spain ; and that the
world of which I speak is different from that in which the
Romans, and Alexander, and the Greeks, made mighty
efforts with great armies to gain the possession of.
Nor have they been affected by the recent noble example of the kings of Portugal, who have had the
courage to explore as far as Guinea, and to make the
discovery of it, expending so much gold and so many
lives in the undertaking, that a calculation of the
population of the kingdom would show, that one half

of them have died in Guinea: and though it is now a long time since they commenced these great exertions, the return for their labour and expense has hitherto been trifling; this people has also dared to make conquests in Africa, and to carry on their exploits to Ceuta, Tangier, Algiers, and Alcazar, repeatedly giving battle to the Moors; and all this at great expense; simply because it was an exploit worthy of a prince, undertaken for the service of God, and to advance the enlargement of His kingdom. The more I said on the subject, the more two-fold was reproach cast upon it, even to the expression of abhorrence, no consideration being given to the honour and fame that accrued to your Highnesses throughout all Christendom, from your Highnesses having undertaken this enterprise; so that there was neither great nor small who did not desire to hear tidings of it. Your Highnesses replied to me encouragingly, and desired that I should pay no regard to those who spoke ill of the undertaking, inasmuch as they had received no authority or countenance whatever from your Highnesses.

I started from San Lucar, in the name of the most Holy Trinity, on Wednesday the 30th of May, much fatigued with my voyage, for I had hoped, when I left the Indies, to find repose in Spain; whereas, on the contrary, I experienced nothing but opposition and vexation. I sailed to the island of Madeira by a circuitous route, in order to avoid any encounter with an armed fleet from France, which was on the look out for me off Cape St Vincent. Thence I went to the Canaries, from which islands I sailed with but one ship and two caravels, having dispatched the other ships to Española by the direct road to the Indies: while

I myself moved southward, with the view of reaching the equinoctial line, and of then proceeding westward, so as to leave the island of Española to the north. But having reached the Cape Verde islands (an incorrect name, for they are so barren that nothing green was to be seen there, and the people so sickly that I did not venture to remain among them), I sailed away four hundred and eighty miles, which is equivalent to a hundred and twenty leagues, towards the south-west, where, when it grew dark, I found the north star to be in the fifth degree. The wind then failed me, and I entered a climate where the intensity of the heat was such, that I thought both ships and men would have been burnt up, and everything suddenly got into such a state of confusion, that no man dared go below deck to attend to the securing of the water-cask and the provisions. This heat lasted eight days; on the first day the weather was fine, but on the seven other days it rained and was cloudy, yet we found no alleviation of our distress; so that I certainly believe, that if the sun had shone as on the first day, we should not have been able to escape in any way.

I recollect, that in sailing towards the Indies, as soon as I passed a hundred leagues to the westward of the Azores, I found the temperature change: and this is so all along from north to south. I determined, therefore, if it should please the Lord to give me a favourable wind and good weather, so that I might leave the part where I then was, that I would give up pursuing the southward course, yet not turn backwards, but sail towards the west, moving in that direction in the hope of finding the same temperature that I had experienced when I sailed in the parallel of the Canaries,—and then, if it proved so, I should still be able to proceed more to the south. At the end of these eight days it pleased our Lord to give me a favourable east wind, and I steered to the west, but did not venture to move lower down towards the south, because I discovered a very great change in the sky and the stars, although I found no alteration in the temperature. I resolved, therefore, to keep on the direct westward course, in a line from Sierra Leone, and not to change it until the chance offered of more speedily reaching land on another tack, which I was very desirous to do, for the purpose of repairing the vessels, and of renewing, if possible, our stock of provisions, and taking in what water we wanted. At the end of seventeen days, during which our Lord gave me a propitious wind, we saw land at noon of Tuesday the 31st of July. This I had expected on the Monday before, and held that route up to this point; but as the sun's strength increased, and our supply of water was failing, I resolved to make for the Carribee Islands, and set sail in that direction; when, by the mercy of God, which He has always extended to me, one of the sailors went up to the main-top and saw to the westward a range of three mountains. Upon this we repeated the "Salve Regina," and other prayers, and all of us gave many thanks to our Lord. I then gave up our northward course, and put in for the land: at the hour of complines we reached a cape, which I called Cape Galea, having already given to the island the name of Trinidad, and here we found a harbour, which would have been excellent but that there was no good anchorage. We saw houses and people on the spot, and the country around was very beautiful, and as

fresh and green as the gardens of Valencia in the month
of March. I was disappointed at not being able to
put into the harbour, and ran along the coast to the
westward. After sailing five leagues I found very
good bottom, and anchored. The next day I set sail
in the same direction, in search of a harbour where I
might repair the vessels and take in water, as well as
improve the stock of provisions which I had brought
out with me. When we had taken in a pipe of water,
we proceeded onwards till we reached the cape, and
there finding good anchorage and protection from the
east wind, I ordered the anchors to be dropped, the
water-cask to be repaired, a supply of water and wood
to be taken in, and the people to rest themselves from
the fatigues which they had endured for so long a time.
I gave to this point the name of Sandy Point (Punta
del Arenal). All the ground in the neighbourhood
was filled with foot-marks of animals, like the impression
of the foot of a goat; but although it would have
appeared from this circumstance that they were very
numerous, only one was seen, and that was dead. On
the following day a large canoe came from the eastward, containing twenty-four men, all in the prime
of life, and well provided with arms, such as bows,
arrows, and wooden shields; they were all, as I have
said, young, well-proportioned, and not dark black,
but whiter than any other Indians that I had seen,—
of very graceful gesture and handsome forms, wearing
their hair long and straight, and cut in the Spanish
style. Their heads were bound round with cotton
scarfs elaborately worked in colours, which resembled
the Moorish head-dresses. Some of these scarfs were
worn round the body and used as a covering in lieu of

trousers. The natives spoke to us from the canoe
while it was yet at a considerable distance, but none
of us could understand them; I made signs to them,
however, to come nearer to us, and more than two hours
were spent in this manner,—but if by any chance they
moved a little nearer, they soon pushed off again.
I caused basins and other shining objects to be shewn
to them to tempt them to come near; and after a
long time, they came somewhat nearer than they had
hitherto done,—upon which, as I was very anxious
to speak with them, and had nothing else to shew
them to induce them to approach, I ordered a drum
to be played upon the quarter-deck, and some of our
young men to dance, believing the Indians would come
to see the amusement. No sooner, however, did they
perceive the beating of the drum and the dancing, than
they all left their oars, and strung their bows, and
each man laying hold of his shield, they commenced
discharging their arrows at us; upon this, the music
and dancing soon ceased, and I ordered a charge to be
made from some of our cross-bows; they then left us,
and went rapidly to the other caravel, and placed themselves under its poop. The pilot of that vessel received
them courteously, and gave to the man who appeared
to be their chief, a coat and hat; and it was then
arranged between them, that he should go to speak
with him on shore. Upon this the Indians immediately
went thither and waited for him; but as he would
not go without my permission, he came to my ship
in the boat, whereupon the Indians got into their canoe
again and went away, and I never saw any more of
them or of any of the other inhabitants of the island.
When I reached the point of Arenal, I found that the

island of Trinidad formed with the land of Gracia a
strait of two leagues' width from east to west, and as
we had to pass through it to go to the north, we found
some strong currents which crossed the strait, and
which made a great roaring, so that I concluded there
must be a reef of sand or rocks, which would preclude
our entrance; and behind this current was another
and another, all making a roaring noise like the sound
of breakers against the rocks. I anchored there, under
the said point of Arenal, outside of the strait, and found
the water rush from east to west with as much impetu-
osity as that of the Guadalquivir at its conflux with
the sea; and this continued constantly day and night,
so that it appeared to be impossible to move backwards
for the current or forwards for the shoals. In the dead
of night, while I was on deck, I heard an awful roaring
that came from the south towards the ship; I stopped
to observe what it might be, and I saw the sea rolling
from west to east like a mountain as high as the ship,
and approaching by little and little; on the top of this
rolling sea came a mighty wave roaring with a frightful
noise, and with all this terrific uproar were other conflicting currents, producing, as I have already said, a
sound as of breakers upon the rocks. To this day
I have a vivid recollection of the dread I then felt, lest
the ship might founder under the force of that tremendous sea; but it passed by, and reached the mouth of
the before-mentioned passage, where the uproar lasted
for a considerable time. On the following day I sent
out boats to take soundings, and found that in the
strait, at the deepest part of the embouchure, there
were six or seven fathoms of water, and that there
were constant contrary currents, one running inwards,

and the other outwards. It pleased the Lord, however, to give us a favourable wind, and I passed through the middle of the strait, after which I recovered my tranquillity. The men happened at this time to draw up some water from the sea, which, strange to say, proved to be fresh. I then sailed northwards till I came to a very high mountain, at about twenty-six leagues from the Punta del Arenal; here two lofty headlands appeared, one towards the east, and forming part of the island of Trinidad, and the other, on the west, being part of the land which I have already called Gracia; we found here a channel still narrower than that of Arenal, with similar currents, and a tremendous roaring of water; the water here also was fresh. Hitherto I had held no communication with any of the people of this country, although I very earnestly desired it; I therefore sailed along the coast westwards, and the further I advanced, the fresher and more wholesome I found the water; and when I had proceeded a considerable distance, I reached a spot where the land appeared to be cultivated. There I anchored, and sent the boats ashore, and the men who went in them found the natives had recently left the place; they also observed that the mountain was covered with monkeys. They came back, and as the coast at that part presented nothing but a chain of mountains, I concluded that further west we should find the land flatter, and consequently in all probability inhabited. Actuated by this thought I weighed anchor, and ran along the coast until we came to the end of the cordillera; I then anchored at the mouth of a river, and we were soon visited by a great number of the inhabitants, who informed us, that the country was called Paria,

and that further westward it was more fully peopled.
I took four of these natives, and proceeded on my
westward voyage; and when I had gone eight leagues
further, I found on the other side of a point which I
called the Needle, one of the most lovely countries in
the world, and very thickly peopled: it was three
o'clock in the morning when I reached it, and seeing
its verdure and beauty, I resolved to anchor there
and communicate with the inhabitants.   Some of the
natives soon came out to the ship, in canoes, to beg me,
in the name of their king, to go on shore; and when
they saw that I paid no attention to them, they came
to the ship in their canoes in countless numbers, many
of them wearing pieces of gold on their breasts, and
some with bracelets of pearls on their arms; on seeing
which I was much delighted, and made many inquiries
with the view of learning where they found them.
They informed me, that they were to be procured in
their own neighbourhood, and also at a spot to the
northward of that place.   I would have remained here,
but the provisions of corn, and wine, and meats, which
I had brought out with so much care, for the people
whom I had left behind, were nearly wasted, so that
all my anxiety was to get them into a place of safety,
and not to stop for any thing.   I wished, however, to
get some of the pearls that I had seen, and with that
view sent the boats on shore.   The natives are very
numerous, and for the most part handsome in person,
and of the same colour as the Indians we had already
seen; they are, moreover, very tractable, and received
our men who went on shore most courteously, seeming
very well disposed towards us.   These men relate,
that when the boats reached shore, two of the chiefs,

The Island of Pearls

whom they took to be father and son, came forward in advance of the mass of the people, and conducted them to a very large house with façades, and not round and tent-shaped as the other houses were; in this house were many seats, on which they made our men sit down, they themselves sitting on other seats. They then caused bread to be brought, with many kinds of fruits, and various sorts of wine, both white and red, not made of grapes, but apparently produced from different fruits. The most reasonable inference is, that they use maize, which is a plant that bears a spine like an ear of wheat, some of which I took with me to Spain, where it now grows abundantly; this they seemed to regard as most excellent, and set a great value upon it. The men remained together at one end of the house, and the women at the other. Great vexation was felt by both parties that they could not understand each other, for they were mutually anxious to make inquiries respecting each other's country. After our men had been entertained at the house of the elder Indian, the younger took them to his house, and gave them an equally cordial reception; after which they returned to their boats and came on board. I weighed anchor forthwith, for I was hastened by my anxiety to save the provisions which were becoming spoiled, and which I had procured and preserved with so much care and trouble, as well as to attend to my own health, which had been affected by long watching; and although on my former voyage, when I discovered terra firma, I passed thirty-three days without natural rest, and was all that time without seeing it, yet never were my eyes so much affected or so painful as at this period. These people, as I have already said, are very graceful in

form,—tall, and elegant in their movements, wearing
their hair very long and smooth, they also bind their
heads with handsome worked handkerchiefs, which
from a distance look like silk or gauze; others use the
same material in a longer form, wound round them
so as to cover them like trousers, and this is done by
both the men and the women. These people are of
a whiter skin than any that I have seen in the Indies.
It is the fashion among all classes to wear something
at the breast, and on the arms, and many wear pieces
of gold hanging low on the bosom. Their canoes are
larger, lighter, and of better build than those of the
islands which I have hitherto seen, and in the middle
of each they have a cabin or room, which I found
was occupied by the chiefs and their wives. I called
this place "Jardines," that is, "the Gardens," for the
place and the people corresponded with that appellation.
I made many inquiries as to where they found the gold,
in reply to which, all of them directed me to an elevated
tract of land at no great distance, on the confines of
their own country, lying to the westward; but they
all advised me not to go there, for fear of being eaten,
and at the time, I imagined that by their description
they wished to imply, that they were cannibals who
dwelt there, but I have since thought it possible,
that they meant merely to express, that the country
was filled with beasts of prey. I also inquired of them
where they obtained the pearls, and in reply to this
question likewise, they directed me to the westward,
and also to the nor h, behind the country they occupied.
I did not put this information to the test, on account
of the provisions, and the weakness of my eyes, and
because the large ship that I had with me was not

calculated for such an undertaking. The short time that I spent with them was all passed in putting questions; and at evening, as I have already said, we returned to the ships, upon which I weighed anchor and sailed to the westward. I proceeded onwards on the following day, until I found that we were only in three fathoms water; at this time I was still under the idea that it was but an island, and that I should be able to make my exit by the north. Upon which I sent a light caravel in advance of us, to see whether there was any exit, or whether the passage was closed; the caravel proceeded a great distance, until it reached a very large gulf, in which there appeared to be four smaller gulfs, from one of which debouched a large river; they invariably found ground at five fathoms, and a great quantity of very fresh water—indeed, I never tasted any equal to it. I felt great anxiety when I found that I could make no exit, either by the north, south, or west, but that I was enclosed on all three sides by land; I therefore weighed anchor, and sailed in a backward direction, with the hope of finding a passage to the north by the strait, which I have already described; but I could not return along the inhabited part where I had already been, an account of the currents, which drove me entirely out of my course. But constantly, at every headland, I found the water sweet and clear, and we were carried eastwards very powerfully towards the two straits already mentioned; I then conjectured, that the currents and the overwhelming mountains of water which rushed into these straits with such an awful roaring, arose from the contest between the fresh water and the sea. The fresh water struggled with the salt to oppose its entrance, and the salt contended against the fresh in its efforts to gain a passage outwards. And I formed the conjecture, that at one time there was a continuous neck of land from the island of Trinidad and with the land of Gracia, where the two straits now are, as your Highnesses will see, by the drawing which accompanies this letter. I passed out by this northern strait, and found the fresh water come even there; and when, by the aid of the wind, I was enabled to proceed, I remarked, while on one of the watery billows which I have described, that in the channel, the water on the inner side of the current was fresh, and on the outside salt.

[Columbus proceeds to state his belief that the world is not quite round, but like a very round pear, having a raised projection for the stalk. He believes that he has arrived near the prominent part, and that the Garden of Eden (or terrestrial paradise) is situated there. From it the torrents of fresh water previously mentioned rush down and form the "lake" (i.e. the Gulf of Paria) between Trinidad and the mainland. These beliefs are supported by elaborate arguments.]

I now return to my subject of the land of Gracia, and of the river and lake found there, which latter might more properly be called a sea; for a lake is but a small expanse of water, which, when it becomes great, deserves the name of a sea, just as we speak of the Sea of Galilee and the Dead Sea; and I think that if the river mentioned does not proceed from the terrestrial paradise, it comes from an immense tract of land situated in the south, of which no knowledge has been hitherto obtained. But the more I reason on the subject, the more satisfied I become that the terrestrial paradise is situated in the spot I have described; and

I ground my opinion upon the arguments and authorities already quoted. May it please the Lord to grant your Highnesses a long life, and health and peace to follow out so noble an investigation; in which I think our Lord will receive great service, Spain considerable increase of its greatness, and all Christians much consolation and pleasure, because by this means the name of our Lord will be published abroad.

In all the countries visited by your Highnesses' ships, I have caused a high cross to be fixed upon every headland, and have proclaimed, to every nation that I have discovered, the lofty estate of your Highnesses, and of your court in Spain. I also tell them all I can respecting our holy faith and of the belief in the holy mother Church, which has its members in all the world; and I speak to them also of the courtesy and nobleness of all Christians, and of the faith they have in the Holy Trinity. May it please the Lord to forgive those who have calumniated and still calumniate this excellent enterprise, and oppose and have opposed its advancement, without considering how much glory and greatness will accrue from it to your Highnesses throughout all the world. They cannot state anything in disparagement of it, except its expense, and that I have not immediately sent back the ships loaded with gold. They speak this without considering the shortness of the time, and how many difficulties there are to contend with; and that every year there are individuals who singly earn by their deserts out of your Majesties' own household, more revenue than would cover the whole of this expense. Nor do they remember that the princes of Spain have never gained possession of any land out of their own country, until now that your

Highnesses have become the masters of another world, where our holy faith may become so much increased, and whence such stores of wealth may be derived; for although we have not sent home ships laden with gold, we have, nevertheless, sent satisfactory samples, both of gold and of other valuable commodities, by which it may be judged that in a short time large profit may be derived. Neither do they take into consideration the noble spirit of the princes of Portugal, who so long ago carried into execution the exploration of Guinea, and still follow it up along the coast of Africa, in which one-half of the population of the country has been employed, and yet the King is more determined on the enterprise than ever. The Lord grant all that I have said, and lead them to think deeply upon what I have written; which is not the thousandth part of what might be written of the deeds of princes who have set their minds upon gaining knowledge, and upon obtaining territory and keeping it.

I say all this, not because I doubt the inclination of your Highnesses to pursue the enterprise while you live,—for I rely confidently on the answers your Highnesses once gave me by word of mouth,—nor because I have seen any change in your Highnesses, but from the fear of what I have heard from those of whom I have been speaking; for I know that water dropping on a stone will at length make a hole. Your Highnesses responded to me with that nobleness of feeling which all the world knows you to possess, and told me to pay no attention to these calumniations; for that your intention was to follow up and support the undertaking, even if nothing were gained by it but stones and sand. Your Highnesses also desired me to be in no way anxious about the expense, for that much greater cost had been incurred on much more trifling matters, and that you considered all the past and future expense as well laid out; for that your Highnesses believed that our holy faith would be increased, and your royal dignity enhanced, and that they were no friends of the royal estate who spoke ill of the enterprise.

And now, during the despatch of the information respecting these lands which I have recently discovered, and where I believe in my soul that the earthly paradise is situated, the "Adelantado" will proceed with three ships, well stocked with provisions, on a further investigation, and will make all the discoveries he can about these parts.   Meanwhile, I shall send your Highnesses this letter, accompanied by a drawing of the country, and your Majesties will determine on what is to be done, and give your orders as to how it is your pleasure that I should proceed: the which, by the aid of the Holy Trinity, shall be carried into execution with all possible diligence, in the faithful service and to the entire satisfaction of your Majesties.   Thanks be to God.

CARTIER. SECOND VOYAGE (1535–1536)

CHAPTER 1

A short and brief narration of the navigation made
by the commandment of the King of France to
the Islands of Canada, Hochelaga, Saguenay, and
divers others, which now are called New France,
with the particular customs and manners of the
inhabitants therein.

In the year of our Lord 1535, upon Whitsunday,
being the 16 of May, by the commandment of our
captain, James Cartier, and with a common accord,
in the Cathedral Church of St Malo we devoutly each
one confessed ourselves and received the Sacrament.
And all entering into the choir of the said church, we
presented ourselves before the Reverend Father in
Christ, the Lord Bishop of St Malo, who blessed us all,
being in his bishop's robes. The Wednesday following,
being the 19 of May, there arose a good gale of wind,
and therefore we hoised sail with three ships; that is
to say, the great *Hermina*, being in burden about a
hundred or a hundred and twenty ton, wherein the
foresaid Captain James Cartier was General, and
Master Thomas Frosmont chief master, accompanied
with Master Claudius de Pont Briand, son to the Lord
of Montcevell, and cup-bearer to the Dauphin of
France, Charles of Pomeray, John Poulet, and other

gentlemen. In the second ship called the little *Hermina*, being of threescore ton burden, were captains under the said Cartier, Mace Jalobert, and Master William Marie. In the third ship called the *Hermerillon*, being of forty ton in burden, were captains Master William Britton, and Master James Maingare.

So we sailed with a good and prosperous wind until the 20 of the said month, at which time the weather turned into storms and tempests, the which, with contrary winds and darkness, endured so long that our ships, being without any rest, suffered as much as any ships that ever went on seas; so that the 25 of June, by reason of that foul and foggy weather, all our ships lost sight one of another again till we came to Newfoundland, where we had appointed to meet. After we had lost one another, we in the General's ship were with contrary winds tossed to and fro on the sea until the seventh of July, upon which day we arrived in Newfoundland, and came to the island called the Island of Birds, which lieth from the mainland fourteen leagues. This island is so full of birds that all our ships might easily have been freighted with them; and yet for the great number that there is, it would not seem that any were taken away. We to victual ourselves filled two boats of them. This island hath the Pole elevated 49 degrees and 40 minutes. Upon the eighth of the said month we sailed further, and with a prosperous weather came to the port called the Port of White Sands, that is in the bay called the Bay of Castles, where we had purposed to meet and stay together the 15 of the month. In this place therefore we looked for our fellows, that is to say, the other two ships, till the 26 of the month, on which day both

came together. So soon as our fellows were come, we
set our ships in a readiness, taking in both water,
wood, and other necessaries. And then on the 29 of
the said month, early in the morning, we hoised sail
to pass on further; and sailing along the northern
coast, that runneth north-east and south-west, till two

Newfoundland and part of the River St Lawrence

hours after sunset or thereabouts, then we crossed
along two islands, which do stretch further forth than
the others, which we called St William's Islands, being
distant about 20 leagues or more from the Port of
Brest. All the coast from the Castles to that place
lieth east and west, north-east and south-west, having

between it sundry little islands, altogether barren and full of stones, without either earth or trees, except certain valleys only. The next day, being the 30 of July, we sailed on westward to find out other islands, which as yet we had not found, twelve leagues and a half. Among which there is a great bay toward the north all full of islands and great creeks, where many good harbours seem to be. Them we named St Martha's Islands, from which about a league and a half further into the sea there is a dangerous shallow, wherein are five rocks, which lie from St Martha's Islands about seven leagues, as you pass into the said islands, on the east and on the west side. To which we came the said day an hour after noon, and from that hour until midnight we sailed about fifteen leagues athwart a cape of the lower islands, which we named St Germain's Islands, south-eastward. From which place about three leagues there is a very dangerous shallow. Likewise between St Germain's Cape and St Martha's, about two leagues from the said islands, there lieth a bank of sand, upon which bank the water is but four fathom deep; and therefore, seeing the danger of the coast, we struck sail and went no further that night. The next day, being the last of July, we went all along the coast that runneth east and west, and somewhat south-easterly, which is all environed about with islands and dry sands, and in truth is very dangerous. The length from St Germain's Cape to the said islands is about 17 leagues and a half; at the end of which there is a goodly plot of ground full of huge and high trees, albeit the rest of the coast be compassed about with sands without any sign or show of harbours, till we came to Cape Thiennot,

which trendeth north-west about seven leagues from
the foresaid islands, which Cape Thiennot we noted
in our former voyage, and therefore we sailed on all
that night west and west-north-west, till it was day,
and then the wind turned against us. Wherefore we
went to seek a haven wherein we might harbour our
ships, and by good hap found one fit for our purpose,
about seven leagues and a half beyond Cape Thiennot,
and that we named St Nicholas Haven. It lieth amidst
four islands that stretch into the sea. Upon the
nearest we for a token set up a wooden cross. But
note by the way that this cross must be brought north-
east, and then bending toward it, leave it on the left
hand and you shall find six fathom water, and within
the haven four. All this coast is full of shoals and
very dangerous, albeit in sight many good havens
seem to be there, yet is there nought else but shelves
and sands.

We stayed and rested ourselves in the said haven
until the eighth of August, being Sunday, on which
day we hoised sail, and came toward land on the south
side toward Cape Rabast, distant from the said haven
about twenty leagues north-north-east and south-south-
west. But the next day there rose a stormy and a
contrary wind; and because we could find no haven
there toward the south, thence we went coasting along
toward the north, beyond the abovesaid haven about
ten leagues, where we found a goodly great gulf, full
of islands, passages, and entrances toward what wind
soever you please to bend. For the knowledge of this
gulf there is a great island that is like to a cape of
land, stretching somewhat further forth than the
others; and about two leagues within the land there

is a hill fashioned as it were a heap of corn. We named the said gulf St Lawrence his Bay.

The fourteenth of the said month we went from the said St Lawrence his Bay, or Gulf, sailing westward, and discovered a cape of land toward the south, that runneth west and by south, distant from the said St Lawrence his Bay about five-and-twenty leagues. And of the two wild men which we took in our former voyage it was told us, that this was part of the southern coast, and that there was an island, on the southerly part of which is the way to go from Honguedo (where the year before we had taken them) to Canada, and that two days' journey from the said cape and island began the kingdom of Saguenay, on the north shore extending toward Canada; and about three leagues athwart the said cape there is above a hundred fathom water. Moreover I believe that there were never so many whales seen as we saw that day about the said cape. The next day after, being our Lady day of August, the fifteenth of the month, having passed the strait, we had notice of certain lands that we left toward the south, which lands are full of very great and high hills. And this cape we named the Island of the Assumption. We trended the said lands about toward the south: from the said day until Tuesday noon following the wind came west, and therefore we bended toward the north, purposing to go and see the land that we before had spied. Being arrived there, we found the said lands, as it were joined together, and low toward the sea; and the northerly mountains that are upon the said low lands stretch east, and west, and a quarter of the south. Our wild men told us that there was the beginning of Saguenay, and that it was land inhabited, and that thence cometh the red copper, of them named *caignetadze*. There is between the southerly lands and the northerly about thirty leagues distance, and more than two hundred fathom depth. The said men did moreover certify unto us that there was the way and beginning of the great river of Hochelaga, and ready way to Canada; which river the further it went the narrower it came, even into Canada, and that then there was fresh water, which went so far upwards, that they had never heard of any man who had gone to the head of it, and that there is no other passage but with small boats. Our captain hearing their talk, and how they did affirm no other passage to be there, would not at that time proceed any further, till he had seen and noted the other lands and coast toward the north, which he had omitted to see from St Lawrence his Gulf, because he would know if between the lands toward the north any passage might be discovered.

CHAPTER 2

How our captain caused the ships to return back again, only to know if in St Lawrence Gulf there were any passage toward the north.

Upon the 18 of August, being Wednesday, our captain caused his ships to wind back, and bend toward the other shore, so that we trended the said northerly coast, which runneth north-east and south-west, being fashioned like unto half a bow, and is a very high land, but yet not so high as that on the south parts. The Thursday following we came to seven very high islands, which we named the Round

Islands. These islands are distant from the south
shore about 40 leagues, and stretch out into the sea
about 3 or 4 leagues. Against these there are goodly
low grounds to be seen, full of goodly trees, which we
the Friday following with our boats compassed about.
Overthwart these lands there are divers sandy shelves,
more than two leagues into the sea, very dangerous,
which at a low water remain almost dry. At the
furthest bounds of these low lands, that contain about
ten leagues, there is a river of fresh water, that with
such swiftness runneth into the sea, that for the space
of one league within it the water is as fresh as any
fountain water. We with our boats entered into the
said river, at the entrance of which we found about
one fathom and a half of water. There are in this
river many fishes shaped like horses, which, as our
wild men told us, all the day long lie in the water,
and the night on land; of which we saw therein a
great number. The next day, being the 21 of the
month, by break of day we hoised sail, and sailed so
long along the said coast that we had sight of the rest
of the said northern coast, which as yet we had not
seen, and of the Island of the Assumption, which we
went to discover, departing from the said land. Which
thing so soon as we had done and that we were certified
no other passage to be there, we came to our ships
again, which we had left at the said islands, where is
a good harbour, the water being about nine or ten
fathom. In the same place by occasion of contrary
winds and foggy mists, we were constrained to stay,
not being either able to come out of it, or hoise sail,
till the 24 of the month. On which day we departed
and came to a haven on the southerly coast about

80 leagues from the said islands. This haven is over against three flat islands that lie amidst the river, because on the midway between those islands and the said haven, toward the north, there is a very great river that runneth between the high and low lands.

Upon the first of September we departed out of the said haven, purposing to go toward Canada; and about 15 leagues from it toward the west and west-south-west, amidst the river there are three islands, over against the which there is a river which runneth swift, and is of a great depth, and it is that which leadeth into the country and kingdom of Saguenay, as by the two wild men of Canada it was told us. This river passeth and runneth along very high and steep hills of bare stone, where very little earth is, and notwithstanding there is great quantity of sundry sorts of trees that grow in the said bare stones, even as upon good and fertile ground; in such sort that we have seen some so great as well would suffice to make a mast for a ship of thirty ton burden, and as green as possibly can be, growing in a stony rock without any earth at all. At the entrance of the said river we met with four boats full of wild men, which, as far as we could perceive, very fearfully came toward us, so that some of them went back again, and the other came as near us as easily they might hear and understand one of our wild men, who told them his name, and then took acquaintance of them, upon whose word they came to us.

The next morning we hoised sail and went thence, sailing further on, where we had notice of a certain kind of fish never before of any man seen or known. They are about the bigness of a porpoise, yet nothing like them, of body well proportioned, headed like greyhounds, altogether as white as snow, without any spot. Within which river there is great quantity of them; they do live altogether between the sea and the fresh water. These people of the country call them *adhothuys*: they told us they were very savoury and good to be eaten. Moreover, they affirm none to be found elsewhere but in the mouth of that river. The sixth of the month, the weather being calm and fair, we went about fifteen leagues more upward into the river, and there lighted on an island that looketh northward, and it maketh a little haven or creek, wherein are many and innumerable great tortoises, continually lying about that island. There are likewise great quantity of the said *adhothuys* taken by the inhabitors of the country, and there is as great a current in that place as is at Bordeaux in France at every tide. This island is in length about three leagues, and in breadth two, and is a goodly and fertile plot of ground, replenished with many goodly and great trees of many sorts. Among the rest there are many filbert trees, which we found hanging full of them, somewhat bigger and better in savour than ours, but somewhat harder, and therefore we called it the Island of Filberts. The seventh of the month, being our Lady's Even, after service we went from that island to go up higher into the river, and came to fourteen islands, seven or eight leagues from the Island of Filberts, where the country of Canada beginneth, one of which islands is ten leagues in length, and five in breadth, greatly inhabited of such men as only live by fishing of such sorts of fishes as the river affordeth, according to the season of them. After we

had cast anchor between the said great island and the
northerly coast, we went on land and took our two
wild men with us, meeting with many of those country
people, who would not at all approach unto us, but
rather fled from us, until our two men began to speak
unto them, telling them that they were Taignoagny
and Domagaia, who so soon as they had taken acquaintance of them began greatly to rejoice, dancing, and
showing many sorts of ceremonies; and many of the
chiefest of them came to our boats and brought many
eels and other sorts of fishes, with two or three burdens
of great millet wherewith they make their bread, and
many great musk melons.   The same day came also
many other boats full of those countrymen and women,
to see and take acquaintance of our two men, all
which were as courteously received and friendly entertained of our captain as possibly could be.   And to
have them the better acquainted with him, and make
them his friends, he gave them many small gifts, but
of small value; nevertheless they were greatly contented
with them.

The next day following, the lord of Canada (whose
proper name was Donnacona, but by the name of Lord
they call him Agouhanna) with twelve boats came
to our ships, accompanied with many people, who,
causing ten of his boats to go back, with the other
two approached unto us with sixteen men.   Then
began the said Agouhanna over against the smallest
of our ships, according to their manner and fashion,
to frame a long oration, moving all his body and
members after a strange fashion, which thing is a
ceremony and sign of gladness and security among
them.   And then coming to the General's ship, where

Taignoagny and Domagaia were, he spake with them
and they with him. Where they began to tell and
show unto him what they had seen in France, and
what good entertainment they had had: hearing
which things the said lord seemed to be very glad
thereof, and prayed our captain to reach him his arm
that he might kiss it, which thing he did: their lord,
taking it, laid it about his neck, for so they use to do
when they will make much of one. Then our captain
entered into Agouhanna's boat, causing bread and
wine to be brought, to make the said lord and his
company to eat and drink, which thing they did,
and were greatly thereby contented and satisfied.
Our captain for that time gave them nothing, because
he looked for a fitter opportunity. These things being
done, each one took leave of others, and the said lord
went with his boats again to his place of abode.

Our captain then caused our boats to be set in order,
that with the next tide he might go up higher into the
river to find some safe harbour for our ships; and we
passed up the river against the stream about ten leagues,
coasting the said island, at the end whereof we found
a goodly and pleasant sound, where is a little river
and haven, where by reason of the flood there is about
three fathom water. This place seemed to us very
fit and commodious to harbour our ships therein, and
so we did very safely. We named it the Holy Cross
(St Croix), for on that day we came thither. Near
unto it there is a village whereof Donnacona is lord,
and there he keepeth his abode. It is called Stadacona, as goodly a plot of ground as possibly may be
seen, and therewithal very fruitful, full of goodly
trees, even as in France, as oaks, elms, ashes, walnut

trees, maple trees, cedars, vines, and white thorns, that bring forth fruit as big as any damsons, and many other sorts of trees, under which groweth as fair tall hemp as any in France, without any seed or any man's work or labour at all. Having considered the place and finding it fit for our purpose, our captain withdrew himself on purpose to return to our ships: but behold, as we were coming out of the river we met coming against us one of the lords of the said village of Stadacona, accompanied with many others, as men, women, and children, who after the fashion of their country, in sign of mirth and joy, began to make a long oration, the women still singing and dancing up to the knees in water. Our captain, knowing their goodwill and kindness toward us, caused the boat wherein they were to come unto him, and gave them certain trifles, as knives and beads of glass, whereat they were marvellous glad; for being gone about three leagues from them, for the pleasure they conceived of our coming we might hear them sing and see them dance, for all they were so far.

Chapter 3

How our captain went to see and note the bigness of
the island, and the nature of it, and then returned
to the ships, causing them to be brought to the
river of the Holy Cross.

After we were come with our boats unto our ships again, our captain caused our barks to be made ready to go on land in the said island, to note the trees that in show seemed so fair, and to consider the nature and quality of it. Which thing we did, and found it

full of goodly trees like to ours. Also we saw many
goodly vines, a thing not before of us seen in those
countries, and therefore we named it Bacchus Island.
It is in length about twelve leagues, in sight very
pleasant, but full of woods, no part of it manured,
unless it be in certain places where a few cottages be
for fishers' dwellings, as before we have said.

The next day we departed with our ships to bring
them to the place of the Holy Cross. And on the
fourteenth of that month we came thither, and the
lord Donnacona, Taignoagny and Domagaia, with
twenty-five boats full of those people, came to meet
us, coming from the place whence we were come, and
going toward Stadacona, where their abiding is. And
all came to our ships, showing sundry and divers
gestures of gladness and mirth, except those two that
we had brought, to wit, Taignoagny and Domagaia,
who seemed to have altered and changed their mind
and purpose; for by no means they would come
unto our ships, albeit sundry times they were earnestly
desired to do it, whereupon we began to mistrust
somewhat. Our captain asked them if, according to
promise, they would go with him to Hochelaga. They
answered yea, for so they had purposed; and then
each one withdrew himself.

The next day, being the fifteenth of the month,
our captain went on shore to cause certain poles and
piles to be driven into the water, and set up, that the
better and safelier we might harbour our ships there.
And many of those country people came to meet us
there, among whom was Donnacona and our two men,
with the rest of their company, who kept themselves
aside under a point or nook of land that is upon the

shore of a certain river, and no one of them came unto us, as the other did that were not on their side. Our captain understanding that they were there, commanded part of our men to follow him, and he went to the said point, where he found Donnacona, Taignoagny, Domagaia, and divers other; and after salutations given on each side, Taignoagny settled himself foremost to speak to our captain, saying that the lord Donnacona did greatly grieve and sorrow that our captain and his men did wear warlike weapons, and they not. Our captain answered, that albeit it did grieve them, yet would not he leave them off, and that (as he knew) it was the manner of France. But for all these words, our captain and Donnacona left not off to speak one to another, and friendly to entertain one another. Then did we perceive that whatsoever Taignoagny spake was only of himself and of his fellow; for that before they departed thence, our captain and Donnacona entered into a marvellous steadfast league of friendship, whereupon all his people at once with a loud voice cast out three great cries (a horrible thing to hear), and each one having taken leave of the other for that day, we went aboard again.

The day following, we brought our two great ships within the river and harbour, where the waters being at the highest are three fathom deep, and at the lowest but half a fathom. We left our pinnace without the road, to the end we might bring it to Hochelaga. So soon as we had safely placed our ships, behold we saw Donnacona, Taignoagny and Domagaia, with more than five hundred persons, men, women, and children, and the said lord with ten or twelve of the chiefest of the country came aboard of our ships; who were all

courteously received and friendly entertained, both of
our captain and of us all, and divers gifts of small
value were given them. Then did Taignoagny tell
our captain that his lord did greatly sorrow that he
would go to Hochelaga, and that he would not by any
means permit that any of them should go with him,
because the river was of no importance. Our captain
answered him, that for all his saying, he would not
leave off his going thither if by any means it were
possible, for that he was commanded by his king to
go as far as possibly he could; and that if he (that is
to say Taignoagny) would go with him as he had
promised, he should be very well entertained, beside
that he should have such a gift given him as he should
well content himself; for he should do nothing else but
go with him to Hochelaga, and come again. To whom
Taignoagny answered that he would not by any means
go, and thereupon they suddenly returned to their
houses.

The next day, being the seventeenth of September,
Donnacona and his company returned, even as at the
first, and brought with him many eels, with sundry
sorts of other fishes, whereof they take great store in
the said river, as more largely hereafter shall be showed.
And as soon as they were come to our ships, according
to their wonted use they began to sing and dance.
This done, Donnacona caused all his people to be set
on the one side; then making a round circle upon the
sand, he caused our captain, with all his people, to
enter thereinto. Then he began to make a long oration,
holding in one of his hands a maiden child of ten or
twelve years old, which he presented unto our captain;
then suddenly began all his people to make three

great shrieks or howls, in sign of joy and league of
friendship. Presently upon that he did present unto
him two other young male children one after another,
but younger than the other, at the giving of which,
even as before, they gave out shrieks and howls very
loud, with other ceremonies. For which presents our
captain gave the said lord great and hearty thanks.
Then Taignoagny told our captain that one of the
children was his own brother, and that the maiden
child was daughter unto the said lord's own sister,
and that the presents were only given him to the end
he should not go to Hochelaga at all. To whom our
captain answered, that if they were only given him
to that intent, if so he would, he should take them
again, for that by no means he would leave his going
off, for as much as he was so commanded of his king.
But concerning this, Domagaia told our captain that
their lord had given him those children as a sign and
token of goodwill and security, and that he was contented to go with him to Hochelaga; upon which talk
great words arose between Taignoagny and Domagaia,
by which we plainly perceived that Taignoagny was
but a crafty knave, and that he intended but mischief
and treason, as well by this deed as others that we
by him had seen.

After that our captain caused the said children to
be put in our ships, and caused two swords and two
copper basins, the one wrought, the other plain, to
be brought unto him, and them he gave to Donnacona,
who was therewith greatly contented, yielding most
hearty thanks unto our captain for them. And
presently upon that he commanded all his people to
sing and dance, and desired our captain to cause a

piece of artillery to be shot off, because Taignoagny
and Domagaia made great brags of it, and had told
them marvellous things, and also because they had
never heard nor seen any before. To whom our
captain answered that he was content; and by and by
he commanded his men to shoot off twelve cannons
charged with bullets into the wood that was hard by
those people and ships; at whose noise they were
greatly astonished and amazed, for they thought that
heaven had fallen upon them, and put themselves to
flight, howling, crying, and shrieking, so that it seemed
hell was broken loose. But before we went thence,
Taignoagny caused other men to tell us that those
men, which we had left in our pinnace in the road,
had slain two men of their company with a piece of
ordnance that they had shot off; whereupon the rest
had put themselves all to flight, as though they should
all have been slain.   Which afterward we found untrue,
because our men had not shot off any piece at all
that day.

Chapter 4

How Donnacona and Taignoagny with others devised
    a pretty sleight or policy: for they caused three
    of their men to be attired like devils, feigning
    themselves to be sent from their god Cudruaigny,
    only to hinder our voyage to Hochelaga.

The next day, being the eighteenth of September,
these men still endeavoured themselves to seek all
means possible to hinder and let our going to Hochelaga,
and devised a pretty guile, as hereafter shall be showed.
They went and dressed three men like devils, being

wrapped in dogs' skins white and black, their faces besmeared as black as any coals, with horns on their heads more than a yard long, and caused them secretly to be put in one of their boats; but came not near our ships as they were wont to do, for they lay hidden within the wood for the space of two hours, looking for the tide, to the end the boat wherein the devils were might approach and come near us. Which, when time was, came, and all the rest issued out of the wood, coming to us, but yet not so near as they were wont to do. There began Taignoagny to salute our captain, who asked him if he would have the boat to come for him; he answered, not for that time, but after a while he would come unto our ships. Then presently came that boat rushing out, wherein the three counterfeit devils were with such long horns on their heads, and the middlemost came making a long oration, and passed along our ships without turning or looking toward us, but with the boat went toward the land. Then did Donnacona with all his people pursue them, and lay hold on the boat and devils, who so soon as the men were come to them, fell prostrate in the boat even as if they had been dead. Then were they taken up and carried into the wood, being but a stone's cast off; then every one withdrew himself into the wood, not one staying behind with us. Where being, they began to make a long discourse, so loud that we might hear them in our ships, which lasted above half an hour, and being ended, we began to espy Taignoagny and Domagaia coming towards us, holding their hands upward joined together, carrying their hats under their upper garment, showing a great admiration. And Taignoagny, looking up to heaven, cried three times:

"Jesus, Jesus, Jesus!"   And Domagaia, doing as his
fellow had done before, cried: "Jesus Maria, James
Cartier!" Our captain hearing them, and seeing their
gestures and ceremonies, asked of them what they
ailed, and what was happened or chanced anew. They
answered that there were very ill tidings befallen,
saying in French, "Nenni est il bon," that is to say,
it was not good. Our captain asked them again what
it was. Then answered they that their god, Cudruaigny, had spoken in Hochelaga, and that he had sent
those three men to show unto them that there was
so much ice and snow in that country, that whosoever
went thither should die. Which words when we
heard, we laughed and mocked them, saying that their
god Cudruaigny was but a fool and a noddy, for he
knew not what he did or said: then bade we them
show his messengers from us that Christ would defend
them all from cold, if they would believe in Him.
Then did they ask of our captain if he had spoken
with Jesus. He answered, no, but that His priests
had, and that He told them they should have fair
weather. Which words when they had heard, they
thanked our captain, and departed toward the wood
to tell those news unto their fellows, who suddenly
came all rushing out of the wood, seeming to be very
glad for those words that our captain had spoken;
and to show that thereby they had had and felt great
joy, so soon as they were before our ships, they all
together gave out three great shrieks, and thereupon
began to sing and dance, as they were wont to do.
But for a resolution of the matter Taignoagny and
Domagaia told our captain that their lord Donnacona
would by no means permit, that any of them should

go with him to Hochelaga, unless he would leave him some hostage to stay with him. Our captain answered them, that if they would not go with him with a good will, they should stay, and that for all them he would not leave off his journey thither.

CHAPTER 5

How our captain, with all his gentlemen and fifty mariners, departed with our pinnace and the two boats from Canada to go to Hochelaga; and also there is described what was seen by the way upon the said river.

The next day, being the nineteenth of September, we hoised sail, and with our pinnace and two boats departed to go up the river with the flood: where on both shores of it we began to see as goodly a country as possibly can with eye be seen; all replenished with very goodly trees, and vines laden as full of grapes as could be, all along the river, which rather seemed to have been planted by man's hand than otherwise. True it is, that because they are not dressed and wrought as they should be, their bunches of grapes are not so great nor sweet as ours. Also we saw all along the river many houses inhabited of fishers, which take all kinds of fishes; and they came with as great familiarity and kindness unto us as if we had been their countrymen, and brought us great store of fish, with other such things as they had, which we exchanged with them for other wares; who, lifting up their hands toward heaven, gave many signs of joy. We stayed at a place called Hochelay, about five-and-twenty leagues from Canada, where the river waxeth very narrow and runneth very swift; wherefore it is very dangerous, not only for that, but also for certain great stones that are therein. Many boats and barks came unto us, in one of which came one of the chief lords of the country, making a long discourse; who being come near us, did by evident signs and gestures show us, that the higher the river went the more dangerous it was, and bade us take heed of ourselves. The said lord presented and gave unto our captain two of his own children, of which our captain took one, being a wench seven or eight years old, the man child he gave him again, because it was too young, for it was but two or three years old. Our captain, as friendly and as courteously as he could, did entertain and receive the said lord and his company, giving them certain small trifles, and so they departed toward the shore again. Afterwards the said lord and his wife came unto Canada to visit his daughter, bringing unto our captain certain small presents.

From the nineteenth until the eight-and-twentieth of September we sailed up along the said river, never losing one hour of time; all which time we saw as goodly and pleasant a country as possible can be wished for, full (as we have said before) of all sorts of goodly trees, that is to say, oaks, elms, walnut trees, cedars, firs, ashes, box, willows, and great store of vines, all as full of grapes as could be, so that if any of our fellows went on shore, they came home laden with them. There are likewise many cranes, swans, geese, ducks, pheasants, partridges, thrushes, blackbirds, turtles, finches, redbreasts, nightingales, sparrows of divers kinds, with many other sorts of birds, even as in France, and great plenty and store.

Upon the 28 of September we came to a great wide lake in the middle of the river, five or six leagues broad and twelve long. All that day we went against the tide, having but two fathom water, still keeping the said scantling. Being come to one of the heads of the lake, we could espy no passage or going out; nay, rather it seemed to have been closed and shut up round about, and there was but a fathom and a half of water, little more or less. And therefore we were constrained to cast anchor and to stay with our pinnace, and went with our two boats to seek some going out, and in one place we found four or five branches, which out of the river came into the lake, and they came from Hochelaga. But in the said branches, because of the great fierceness and swiftness wherewith they break out, and the course of the water, they make certain bars and shoals, and at that time there was but a fathom water. Those shoals being passed, we found four or five fathom, and as far as we could perceive by the flood, it was that time of the year that the waters are lowest, for at other times they flow higher by three fathoms. All these four or five branches do compass about five or six islands, very pleasant, which make the head of the lake: about fifteen leagues beyond they do all come into one. That day we landed in one of the said islands, and met with five men that were hunting of wild beasts, who as freely and familiarly came to our boats without any fear, as if we had ever been brought up together. Our boats being somewhat near the shore, one of them took our captain in his arms and carried him on shore, as lightly and easily as if he had been a child of five years old, so strong and sturdy was this fellow. We found

that they had a great heap of wild rats that live in
the water, as big as a coney, and very good to eat,
which they gave unto our captain, who for a recompense gave them knives and glass beads. We asked
them with signs if that was the way to Hochelaga;
they answered, yea, and that we had yet three days'
sailing thither.

Chapter 6

How our captain caused our boats to be mended and
dressed to go to Hochelaga: and because the
way was somewhat difficult and hard, we left our
pinnace behind: and how we came thither, and
what entertainment we had of the people.

The next day our captain, seeing that for that time
it was not possible for our pinnace to go on any further,
caused our boats to be made ready, and as much
munition and victuals to be put in them as they could
well bear. He departed with them, accompanied with
many gentlemen, that is to say, Claudius de Pont
Briand, cup-bearer to the Lord Dauphin of France,
Charles of Pomeray, John Gouion, John Poulet, with
twenty and eight mariners; and Mace Jalobert, and
William Britton, who had the charge under the captain
of the other two ships, to go up as far as they could
into that river. We sailed with good and prosperous
weather until the second of October, on which day we
came to the town of Hochelaga, distant from the place
where we had left our pinnace five-and-forty leagues.
In which place of Hochelaga, and all the way we went,
we met with many of those countrymen, who brought
us fish and such other victuals as they had, still dancing

and greatly rejoicing at our coming. Our captain, to lure them in, and to keep them our friends, to recompense them gave them knives, beads, and such small trifles, wherewith they were greatly satisfied.

So soon as we were come near Hochelaga, there came to meet us above a thousand persons, men, women, and children, who afterward did as friendly and merrily entertain and receive us as any father would do his child, which he had not of long time seen, the men dancing on one side, the women on another, and likewise the children on another. After that they brought us great store of fish, and of their bread made of millet, casting them into our boats so thick that you would have thought it to fall from heaven. Which when our captain saw, he with many of his company went on shore. So soon as ever we were a-land they came clustering about us, making very much of us, bringing their young children in their arms, only to have our captain and his company to touch them, making signs and shows of great mirth and gladness that lasted more than half an hour. Our captain, seeing their loving-kindness and entertainment of us, caused all the women orderly to be set in array, and gave them beads made of tin, and other such small trifles, and to some of the men he gave knives. Then he returned to the boats to supper, and so passed that night, all which while all those people stood on the shore as near our boats as they might, making great fires, and dancing very merrily, still crying, "Aguiaze," which in their tongue signifieth mirth and safety.

CHAPTER 7

How our captain, with five gentlemen and twenty
  armed men all well in order, went to see the town
  of Hochelaga, and the situation of it.

Our captain the next day, very early in the morning,
having very gorgeously attired himself, caused all his
company to be set in order to go to see the town and
habitation of those people, and a certain mountain
that is somewhat near the city: with whom went also
five gentlemen and twenty mariners, leaving the rest
to keep and look to our boats.   We took with us three
men of Hochelaga to bring us to the place.   All along
as we went we found the way as well beaten and
frequented as can be, the fairest and best country that
possibly can be seen, full of as goodly great oaks as
are in any wood in France, under which the ground
was all covered over with fair acorns.   After we had
gone about four or five miles, we met by the way one
of the chiefest lords of the city, accompanied with
many more, who, so soon as he saw us, beckoned and
made signs upon us, that we must rest us in that place,
where they had made a great fire, and so we did.   After
that we had rested ourselves there a while, the said
lord began to make a long discourse, even as we have
said above they are accustomed to do in sign of mirth
and friendship, showing our captain and all his company
a joyful countenance and goodwill; who gave him
two hatchets, a pair of knives, and a cross, which he
made him to kiss, and then put it about his neck, for
which he gave our captain hearty thanks.   This done,
we went along, and about a mile and a half farther

we began to find goodly and large fields, full of such corn as the country yieldeth. It is even as the millet of Bresil, as great and somewhat bigger than small peason, wherewith they live even as we do with ours. In the midst of those fields is the city of Hochelaga, placed near, and as it were joined to a great mountain that is tilled round about, very fertile, on the top of which you may see very far. We named it Mount Royal.

The city of Hochelaga is round, compassed about with timber, with three courses of rampires, one within another, framed like a sharp spire, but laid across above. The rampires are framed and fashioned with pieces of timber laid along on the ground, very well and cunningly joined together after their fashion. This enclosure is in height about two rods. It hath but one gate or entry thereat, which is shut with piles, stakes, and bars. Over it, and also in many places of the wall, there be places to run along, and ladders to get up, all full of stones for the defence of it. There are in the town about fifty houses, about fifty paces long, and twelve or fifteen broad, built all of wood, covered over with the bark of the wood, as broad as any board, very finely and cunningly joined together. Within the said houses there are many rooms, lodgings, and chambers. In the midst of every one there is a great court, in the middle whereof they make their fire. They live in common together; then do the husbands, wives, and children, each one, retire themselves to their chambers. They have also on the top of their houses certain garrets, wherein they keep their corn to make their bread withal: they call it *carraconny*, which they make as hereafter shall follow. They have certain pieces of wood, made hollow like those whereon we beat our hemp, and with certain beetles of wood they beat their corn to powder. Then they make paste of it, and of the paste, cakes or wreaths; then they lay them on a broad and hot stone, and then cover it with hot stones, and so they bake their bread, instead of ovens. They make also sundry sorts of pottage with the said corn, and also of peas and of beans, whereof they have great store, as also with other fruits, as musk melons, and very great cucumbers. They have also in their houses certain vessels as big as any butt or tun, wherein they preserve and keep their fish, causing the same in summer to be dried in the sun, and live therewith in winter, whereof they make great provision, as we by experience have seen. All their viands and meats are without any taste or savour of salt at all. They sleep upon barks of trees laid all along upon the ground, being overspread with the skins of certain wild beasts, wherewith they also clothe and cover themselves.

The thing most precious that they have in all the world they call *esurgny*. It is as white as any snow: they take it in the said river of Cornibotz in the manner following. When any one hath deserved death, or that they take any of their enemies in wars, first they kill him, then with certain knives they give great slashes and strokes upon their flanks, thighs, and shoulders; then they cast the same body so mangled down to the bottom of the river, in a place where the said *esurgny* is, and there leave it ten or twelve hours, then they take it up again, and in the cuts they find the said *esurgny* or *cornibotz*. Of them they make beads, and wear them about their necks, even as we do chains of gold and silver, accounting it the preciousest thing in the world. They have this virtue and property in them, they will stop or staunch bleeding at the nose, for we have proved it. These people are given to no other exercise, but only to husbandry and fishing for their sustenance. They have no care of any other wealth or commodity in this world, for they have no knowledge of it, and that is because they never travel and go out of their country, as those of Canada and Saguenay do, albeit the Canadians with eight or nine villages more alongst that river be subjects unto them.

CHAPTER 8

How we came to the town of Hochelaga, and the entertainment which there we had, and of certain gifts which our captain gave them, with divers other things.

So soon as we were come near the town, a great number of the inhabitants thereof came to present themselves before us after their fashion, making very much of us. We were by our guides brought into the midst of the town. They have in the middlemost part of their houses a large square place, being from side to side a good stone's cast, whither we were brought, and there with signs were commanded to stay. Then suddenly all the women and maidens of the town gathered themselves together, part of which had their arms full of young children, and as many as could came to rub our faces, our arms, and what part of the body soever they could touch, weeping for very joy that they saw us, showing us the best countenance that possibly they could, desiring us with their signs that it would please us to touch their children. That done, the men caused the women to withdraw themselves back; then they every one sat down on the ground round about us, as if they would have shown and rehearsed some comedy or other show. Then presently came the women again, every one bringing a four-square mat in manner of carpets, and spreading them abroad on the ground in that place, they caused us to sit upon them.

That done, the lord and king of the country was brought upon nine or ten men's shoulders (whom in their tongue they call Agouhanna), sitting upon a great stag's skin, and they laid him down upon the foresaid mats near to the captain, every one beckoning unto us that he was their lord and king. This Agouhanna was a man about fifty years old. He was no whit better apparelled than any of the rest, only excepted that he had a certain thing made of the skins of hedgehogs, like a red wreath, and that was instead of his crown. He was full of the palsy, and his members shrunk together. After he had with certain signs saluted our captain and all his company, and by manifest tokens bid all welcome, he showed his legs and arms to our captain, and with signs desired him to touch them; and so he did, rubbing them with his own hands. Then did Agouhanna take the wreath or crown he had about his head, and gave it unto our captain. That done, they brought before him divers diseased men, some blind, some cripple, some lame and impotent, and some so old that the hair of their eyelids came down and covered their cheeks, and laid them all along before our captain, to the end they might of him be touched: for it seemed unto them that God was descended and come down from heaven to heal them.

Our captain seeing the misery and devotion of this poor people, recited the Gospel of St John (that is to say, "In the beginning was the Word"), touching every one that were diseased, praying to God that it would please Him to open the hearts of this poor people, and to make them know His Holy Word, and that they might receive baptism and christendom. That done, he took a Service-book in his hand, and with a loud voice read all the passion of Christ, word by word, that all the standers-by might hear him. All which while this poor people kept silence, and were marvellously attentive, looking up to heaven, and imitating us in gestures. Then he caused the men all orderly to be set on one side, the women on another, and likewise the children on another; and to the chiefest of them he gave hatchets, to the other knives, and to the women beads, and such other small trifles. Then where the children were, he cast rings, counters, and brooches made of tin, whereat they seemed to be very glad. That done, our captain commanded trumpets and other musical instruments to be sounded, which when they heard they were very merry.

Then we took our leave, and went to our boat. The women seeing that, put themselves before to stay us, and brought us out of their meats that they had made ready for us, as fish, pottage, beans, and such other things, thinking to make us eat and dine in that place: but because the meats had no savour at all of salt, we liked them not; but thanked them, and with signs gave them to understand that we had no need to eat.

When we were out of the town, divers of the men and women followed us, and brought us to the top of

the foresaid mountain which we named Mount Royal.
It is about a league from the town.   When as we
were at the top of it, we might discern and plainly
see thirty leagues about.   On the north side of it there
are many hills to be seen running west and east, and
as many more on the south, amongst and between
the which the country is as fair and as pleasant as
possibly can be seen, being level, smooth and very
plain, fit to be husbanded and tilled.   And in the
midst of those fields we saw the river further up a great
way than where we had left our boats; where was the
greatest and the swiftest fall of water that anywhere
hath been seen, and as great, wide, and large as our
sight might discern, going south-west along three fair
and round mountains that we saw, as we judged,
about fifteen leagues from us.   Those which brought
us thither told and showed us that in the said river
there were three such falls of water more, as that was,
where we had left our boats; but because we could
not understand their language, we could not know
how far they were one from another.   Moreover they
showed us with signs that the said three falls being
passed, a man might sail the space of three months
more alongst that river; and that along the hills
that are on the north side, there is a great river which
(even as the other) cometh from the west.   We thought
it to be the river that runneth through the country of
Saguenay.   And without any sign or question moved
or asked of them, they took the chain of our captain's
whistle, which was of silver, and the dagger-haft of one
of our fellow mariners, hanging on his side, being of
yellow copper gilt, and showed us that such stuff came
from the said river, and that there be "*Agouionda*,"

that is as much to say as evil people, who go all
armed even to their fingers' ends. Also they showed
us the manner and making of their armour : they are
made of cords and wood, finely and cunningly wrought
together. They gave us also to understand that those
agouionda do continually war one against another,
but because we did not understand them well, we could
not perceive how far it was to that country. Our
captain showed them red copper, which in their language
they call *caignetadze*, and looking toward that country
with signs asked them if any came from thence ; they
shaking their heads answered "No" : but they showed
us that it came from Saguenay, and that lieth clean
contrary to the other.

After we had heard and seen these things of them,
we drew to our boats, accompanied with a great multitude of those people : some of them whenas they saw
any of our fellows weary, would take them up on their
shoulders, and carry them as on horseback. So soon
as we came to our boats we hoised sail to go toward
our pinnace, doubting of some mischance. Our
departure grieved and displeased them very much,
for they followed us along the river as far as they could.
We went so fast that on Monday, being the fourth
of October, we came where our pinnace was. The
Tuesday following, being the fifth of the month, we
hoised sail, and with our pinnace and boats departed
from thence toward the province of Canada, to the
port of the Holy Cross, where we had left our ships.
The seventh day we came against a river that cometh
from the north, and entered into that river, at the
entrance whereof are four little islands full of fair and
goodly trees. We named that river the river of

Fovetz. But because one of those islands stretcheth itself a great way into the river, our captain at the point of it caused a goodly great cross to be set up, and commanded the boats to be made ready, that with the next tide he might go up the said river and consider the quality of it. Which we did, and that day went up as far as we could; but because we found it to be of no importance, and very shallow, we returned and sailed down the river.

CHAPTER 9

How we came to the port of the Holy Cross, and in
what state we found our ships: and how the lord
of the country came to visit our captain and our
captain him: and of certain particular customs
of the people.

Upon Monday, being the eleventh of October, we came to the port of the Holy Cross, where our ships were, and found that the masters and mariners we had left there had made and reared a trench before the ships, altogether closed with great pieces of timber set upright and very well fastened together. Then had they beset the said trench about with pieces of artillery and other necessary things to shield and defend themselves from the power of all the country. So soon as the lord of the country heard of our coming, the next day, being the twelfth of October, he came to visit us, accompanied with Taignoagny, Domagaia, and many others, feigning to be very glad of our coming, making much of our captain, who as friendly as he could entertained them, albeit they had not deserved it. Donnacona their lord desired our captain the next day

to come and see Canada, which he promised to do.
For the next day, being the thirteenth of the month,
he, with all his gentlemen and fifty mariners very
well appointed, went to visit Donnacona and his
people, about a league from our ships.   The place
where they make their abode is called Stadacona.

When we were about a stone's cast from their
houses, many of the inhabitants came to meet us,
being all set in a rank, and (as their custom is) the
men all on one side, and the women on the other, still
dancing and singing without any ceasing.   And after
we had saluted and received one another, our captain
gave them knives and such other slight things; then
he caused all the women and children to pass along
before him, giving each one a ring of tin, for which
they gave him hearty thanks.   That done, our captain
was by Donnacona and Taignoagny brought to see their
houses, which (the quality considered) were very well
provided and stored with such victuals as the country
yieldeth, to pass away the winter withal.   Then they
showed us the skins of five men's heads, spread upon
boards as we do use parchment.   Donnacona told us
that they were skins of Toudamans, a people dwelling
toward the south, who continually do war against
them.   Moreover, they told us that it was two years
past that those Toudamans came to assault them,
yea even into the said river, in an island that lieth
over against Saguenay, where they had been the night
before, as they were going a-warfaring in Hognedo,
with two hundred persons, men, women, and children;
who being all asleep in a fort that they had made,
they were assaulted by the said Toudamans, who put
fire round about the fort, and as they would have come

out of it to save themselves, they were all slain, only
five excepted, who escaped.   For which loss they yet
sorrowed, showing with signs that one day they would
be revenged.   That done, we came to our ships again.

CHAPTER 10

The manner how the people of that country live : and
    of certain conditions : and of their faith, manners,
    and customs.

This people believe no whit in God, but in one
whom they call Cudruaigny.   They say that often he
speaketh with them, and telleth them what weather shall
follow, whether good or bad.   Moreover, they say that
when he is angry with them he casteth dust into their
eyes.   They believe that when they die they go into
the stars, and thence by little and little descend down
into the horizon, even as the stars do, and that then
they go into certain green fields full of goodly, fair,
and precious trees, flowers, and fruits.   After that
they had given us these things to understand, we
showed them their error, and told that their Cudruaigny
did but deceive them, for he is but a devil and an evil
spirit, affirming unto them that there is but one only
God, who is in heaven, and who giveth us all necessaries,
being the Creator of all Himself, and that only we
must believe in Him : moreover, that it is necessary
for us to be baptized, otherwise we are damned into
hell.   These and many other things concerning our
faith and religion we showed them, all which they
did easily believe, calling their Cudruaigny, *agouiada*
(that is to say, nought), so that very earnestly they
desired and prayed our captain that he would cause

them to be baptized; and their lord, and Taignoagny, Domagaia, and all the people of the town came unto us, hoping to be baptized. But because we did not throughly know their mind, and that there was nobody could teach them our belief and religion, we excused ourselves, desiring Taignoagny and Domagaia to tell the rest of their countrymen that we would come again another time and bring priests and chrism with us, for without them they could not be baptized. Which they did easily believe, for Domagaia and Taignoagny had seen many children baptized in Brittany whiles they were there. Which promise when they heard, they seemed to be very glad.

They live in common together, and of such commodities as their country yieldeth they are indifferently well stored. The inhabitants of the country clothe themselves with the skins of certain wild beasts, but very miserably. In winter they wear hosen and shoes made of wild beasts' skins, and in summer they go barefooted. They keep and observe the rites of matrimony, saving that everyone weddeth two or three wives, which (their husbands being dead) do never marry again, but for the death of their husbands wear a certain black weed all the days of their life, besmearing all their faces with coal dust and grease mingled together as thick as the back of a knife, and by that they are known to be widows.

They are no men of great labour. They dig their grounds with certain pieces of wood as big as half a sword, on which ground groweth their corn, which they call *offici*: it is as big as our small peason: there is great quantity of it growing in Bresil. They have great store of musk melons, pompions, gourds, cucum-

bers, peason and beans of every colour, yet differing
from ours.   There groweth also a certain kind of herb,
whereof in summer they make great provision for all
the year, making great account of it; and only men
use of it.   And first they cause it to be dried in the
sun, then wear it about their necks wrapped in a little
beast's skin made like a little bag, with a hollow piece
of stone or wood like a pipe.   Then when they please
they make powder of it, and then put it in one of the
ends of the said cornet or pipe, and laying a coal of
fire upon it, at the other end suck so long, that they
fill their bodies full of smoke, till that it cometh out
of their mouth and nostrils, even as out of the tunnel
of a chimney.   They say that this doth keep them
warm and in health: they never go without some of
it about them.   We ourselves have tried the same
smoke, and having put it in our mouths, it seemed
almost as hot as pepper.

The women of that country do labour much more
than the men, as well in fishing (whereto they are greatly
given) as in tilling and husbanding their grounds, and
other things.   As well the men as women and children
are very much more able to resist cold than savage
beasts, for we with our own eyes have seen some of
them, when it was coldest (which cold was extreme
raw and bitter), come to our ships stark naked, going
upon snow and ice; which thing seemeth incredible
to them that have not seen it.   Whenas the snow and
ice lieth on the ground, they take great store of wild
beasts, as fawns, stags, bears, martens, hares and
foxes, with divers other sorts, whose flesh they eat raw,
having first dried it in the sun or smoke, and so they
do their fish.   As far forth as we could perceive and

understand by these people, it were a very easy thing
to bring them to some familiarity and civility, and
make them learn what one would. The Lord God for
His mercy's sake set thereunto His helping hand when
He seeth cause. Amen.

CHAPTER 11

Of the greatness and depth of the said river, and of
the sorts of beasts, birds, fishes, and other things
that we have seen, with the situation of the place.

The said river beginneth beyond the Island of the
Assumption, over against the high mountains of
Hognedo and of the Seven Islands. The distance over
from one side to the other is about thirty-five or forty
leagues. In the midst it is above 200 fathom deep.
The surest way to sail upon it is on the south side. And
toward the north, that is to say from the said Seven
Islands, from side to side, there is seven leagues distance,
where are also two great rivers that come down from
the hills of Saguenay, and make divers very dangerous
shelves in the sea. At the entrance of those two
rivers we saw many and great store of whales and
sea-horses. Overthwart the said islands there is
another little river, that runneth along those marish
grounds about three or four leagues, wherein there is
great store of water fowls. From the entrance of
that river to Hochelaga there is about three hundred
leagues distance: the original beginning of it is in
the river that cometh from Saguenay, which riseth
and springeth among high and steep hills. It entereth
into that river before it cometh to the province of
Canada, on the north side. That river is very deep,

high, and strait, wherefore it is very dangerous for
any vessel to go upon it.   After that river followeth the
province of Canada, wherein are many people dwelling
in open boroughs and villages.   There are also in the
circuit and territory of Canada, along and within the
said river, many other islands, some great and some
small, among which there is one that containeth above
ten leagues in length, full of goodly and high trees,
and also many vines.   You may go into it from both
sides, but yet the surest passage is on the south side.
On the shore or bank of that river westward, there is
a goodly, fair, and delectable bay or creek, convenient
and fit for to harbour ships.   Hard by there is in that
river one place very narrow, deep, and swift-running,
but it is not passing the third part of a league; over
against the which there is a goodly high piece of land,
with a town therein: and the country about it is very
well tilled and wrought, and as good as possibly can
be seen.   That is the place and abode of Donnacona,
and of our two men we took in our first voyage: it
is called Stadacona.   But before we come to it, there
are four other peopled towns, that is to say, Ayraste,
Starnatan, Tailla, which standeth upon a hill, Scitadin,
and then Stadacona; under which town, toward the
north, the river and port of the Holy Cross is, where
we stayed from the 15 of September until the 16 of
May, 1536, and there our ships remained dry, as we
have said before.   That place being passed, we found
the habitation of the people called Teguenondahi,
standing upon a high mountain, and the valley of
Hochelay, which standeth in a champaign country.
All the said country on both sides of the river, as far
as Hochelay and beyond, is as fair and plain as ever

was seen. There are certain mountains far distant
from the said river, which are to be seen above the
foresaid towns; from which mountains divers rivers
descend, which fall into the said great river. All
that country is full of sundry sorts of wood and many
vines, unless it be about the places that are inhabited,
where they have pulled up the trees to till and labour
the ground, and to build their houses and lodgings.
There is great store of stags, deer, bears, and other
such like sorts of beasts, as coneys, hares, martens,
foxes, otters, beavers, weasels, badgers, and rats
exceeding great, and divers other sorts of wild beasts.
They clothe themselves with the skins of those beasts,
because they have nothing else to make them apparel
withal. There are also many sorts of birds, as cranes,
swans, bustards, wild geese white and grey, ducks,
thrushes, blackbirds, turtles, wild pigeons, linnets,
finches, redbreasts, stares, nightingales, sparrows, and
other birds, even as in France. Also, as we have said
before, the said river is the plentifullest of fish that
ever hath of any man been seen or heard of, because
that from the mouth to the end of it, according to their
seasons, you shall find all sorts of fresh water fish and
salt. There are also many whales, porpoises, sea-
horses, and *adhothuys*, which is a kind of fish that we
had never seen nor heard of before. They are as
great as porpoises, as white as any snow, their body
and head fashioned as a greyhound: they are wont
always to abide between the fresh and salt water,
which beginneth between the river of Saguenay and
Canada.

Chapter 12

*Of certain advertisements and notes given unto us by
those countrymen, after our return from Hochelaga.*

After our return from Hochelaga we dealt, trafficked,
and with great familiarity and love were conversant
with those that dwelt nearest unto our ships; except
that sometimes we had strife and contention with
certain naughty people, full sore against the will of
the others.

We understood of Donnacona and of others that
the said river is called the river of Saguenay, and
goeth to Saguenay, being somewhat more than a
league farther west-north-west, and that eight or nine
days' journey beyond, it will bear but small boats.
But the right and ready way to Saguenay is up that
river to Hochelaga, and then into another that cometh
from Saguenay, and then entereth into the foresaid
river, and that there is yet one month's sailing thither.
Moreover, they told us and gave us to understand that
there are people clad with cloth as we are, very honest,
and many inhabited towns, and that they have great
store of gold, and red copper; and that about the
land beyond the said first river to Hochelaga and
Saguenay is an island environed round about with that
and other rivers, and that beyond Saguenay the said
river entereth into two or three great lakes, and that
there is a sea of fresh water found, and as they have
heard say of those of Saguenay, there was never man
heard of that found out the end thereof: for, as they
told us, they themselves were never there.

Moreover, they told us that where we had left our pinnace when we went to Hochelaga, there is a river that goeth south-west, from whence there is a whole month's sailing to go to a certain land where there is neither ice nor snow seen, where the inhabitants do continually war one against another, where is great store of oranges, almonds, nuts, and apples, with many other sorts of fruits, and that the men and women are clad with beasts' skins, even as they. We asked them if there were any gold or red copper: they answered no. I take this place to be toward Florida, as far as I could perceive and understand by their signs and tokens.

Chapter 13

Of a strange and cruel disease that came to the people
of Stadacona, wherewith because we did haunt
their company, we were so infected that there
died twenty-five of our company.

In the month of December we understood that the pestilence was come among the people of Stadacona, in such sort, that before we knew of it, according to their confession, there were dead above fifty. Whereupon we charged them neither to come near our fort nor about our ships, or us. And albeit we had driven them from us, the said unknown sickness began to spread itself amongst us after the strangest sort that ever was either heard of or seen; insomuch as some did lose all their strength, and could not stand on their feet; then did their legs swell, their sinews shrink as black as any coal, and their teeth did also almost all fall out.

With such infection did this sickness spread itself
in our three ships, that about the middle of February,
of a hundred and ten persons that we were, there were
not ten whole; so that one could not help the other,
a most horrible and pitiful case considering the place
we were in, forsomuch as the people of the country
would daily come before our fort, and saw but few of
us.   There were already eight dead, and more than
fifty sick, and as we thought, past all hope of recovery.
Our captain seeing this our misery, and that the sickness
was gone so far, ordained and commanded that every
one should devoutly prepare himself to prayer, and in
remembrance of Christ, caused His image to be set
upon a tree, about a flight shot from the fort, amidst the
ice and snow, giving all men to understand that on
the Sunday following, Service should be said there,
and that whosoever could go, sick or whole, should
go thither in procession, singing the seven psalms of
David, with other litanies, praying most heartily that it
would please the said our Christ to have compassion
upon us.   Service being done, and as well celebrated as
we could, our captain there made a vow, that if it
would please God to give him leave to return into
France, he would go on pilgrimage to our Lady of
Rocquemado.

In such sort did the sickness continue and increase,
that there were not above three sound men in the
ships, and none was able to go under hatches to draw
drink for himself nor for his fellows.   Sometimes we
were constrained to bury some of the dead under the
snow, because we were not able to dig any graves for
them, the ground was so hard frozen, and we so weak.
Besides this, we did greatly fear that the people of the

country would perceive our weakness and misery;
which to hide, our captain (whom it pleased God always
to keep in health) would go out with two or three
of the company, some sick and some whole; whom
when he saw out of the fort, he would throw stones
at them and chide them, feigning that so soon as he
came again, he would beat them, and then with signs
show the people of the country that he caused all
his men to work and labour in the ships, some in
caulking them, some in beating of chalk, some in one
thing, and some in another; and that he would not have
them come forth till their work was done. And to
make his tale seem true and likely, he would make all
his men, whole and sound, to make a great noise with
knocking sticks, stones, hammers, and other things
together. At which time we were so oppressed and
grieved with that sickness, that we had lost all hope
ever to see France again, if God of His infinite goodness
and mercy had not with His pitiful eye looked upon
us, and revealed a singular and excellent remedy
against all diseases unto us, the best that ever was
found upon earth, as hereafter shall follow.

CHAPTER 14

How long we stayed in the port of the Holy Cross
amidst the snow and ice, and how many died of
the said disease, from the beginning of it to the
midst of March.

From the midst of November until the midst of
March, we were kept in amidst the ice above two
fathoms thick, and snow above four foot high and
more, higher than the sides of our ships: which lasted

till that time in such sort, that all our drinks were
frozen in the vessels, and the ice through all the ships
was above a hand-breadth thick, as well above hatches
as beneath; and so much of the river as was fresh,
even to Hochelaga, was frozen. In which space there
died five-and-twenty of our best and chiefest men,
and all the rest were so sick that we thought they
should never recover again, only three or four excepted.
Then it pleased God to cast His pitiful eye upon us,
and send us the knowledge of remedy of our healths
and recovery, in such manner as in the next chapter
shall be showed.

CHAPTER 15

How by the grace of God we had notice of a certain
   tree, whereby we all recovered our health: and
   the manner how to use it.

Our captain considering our estate (and how that
sickness was increased and hot amongst us), one day
went forth of the fort, and walking upon the ice, he
saw a troop of those countrymen coming from Stadacona, among which was Domagaia, who not passing ten
or twelve days afore, had been very sick with that
disease, and had his knees swollen as big as a child of
two years old, all his sinews shrunk together, and his
teeth spoiled. Our captain seeing him whole and
sound, was thereat marvellous glad, hoping to understand and know of him how he had healed himself,
to the end he might ease and help his men. So soon
as they were come near him, he asked Domagaia how
he had done to heal himself: he answered, that he had
taken the juice and sap of the leaves of a certain tree,

and therewith had healed himself; for it was a singular remedy against that disease. Then our captain asked of him if any were to be had thereabout, desiring him to show him, for to heal a servant of his, who whilst he was in Canada with Donnacona was stricken with that disease. That he did because he would not show the number of his sick men. Domagaia straight sent two women to fetch some of it, which brought ten or twelve branches of it, and therewithal showed the way how to use it. And that is thus: to take the bark and leaves of the said tree and boil them together, then to drink of the said decoction every other day, and to put the dregs of it upon his legs that is sick: moreover, they told us that the virtue of that tree was to heal any other disease. The tree is in their language called *ameda* or *hanneda*; this is thought to be the sassafras tree.

Our captain presently caused some of that drink to be made for his men to drink of it, but there was none durst taste of it, except one or two, who ventured the drinking of it only to taste and prove it. The others seeing that, did the like, and presently recovered their health, and were delivered of that sickness, and what other disease soever. After this medicine was found and proved to be true, there was such strife about it, who should be first to take of it, that they were ready to kill one another; so that a tree as big as any oak in France was spoiled and lopped bare, and occupied all in five or six days. And it wrought so well, that if all the physicians of Montpellier and Louvain had been there with all the drugs of Alexandria, they would not have done so much in one year as that tree did in six days; for it did so prevail, that as many as used of it, by the grace of God recovered their health.

Chapter 16

How the lord Donnacona, accompanied with Taignoagny and divers others, feigning that they would
go to hunt stags, and deer, tarried out two months,
and at their return brought a great multitude of
people with them, that we were not wont to see
before.

While that disease lasted in our ships, the lord
Donnacona, Taignoagny, with many others, went from
home, feigning that they would go to catch stags and
deer, which are in their tongue called *ajounesta* and
asquenoudo, because the ice and snow was not so broken
along the river that they could sail. It was told us
of Domagaia and others that they would stay out but
a fortnight, and we believed it; but they stayed above
two months, which made us mistrust they had been
gone to raise the country to come against us, and do
us some displeasure, we seeing ourselves so weak and
faint. Albeit we had used such diligence and policy
in our fort, that if all the power of the country had
been about it, they could have done nothing but look
upon us. And whilst they were forth, many of the
people came daily to our ships, and brought us fresh
meat, as stags, deer, fishes, with divers other things,
but held them at such an excessive price, that rather
than they would sell them anything cheap, many
times they would carry them back again, because
that year the winter was very long, and they had some
scarcity and need of them.

CHAPTER 17

How Donnacona came to Stadacona again with a
    great number of people, and because he would
    not come to visit our captain, feigned himself
    to be sore sick, which he did only to have the
    captain come see him.

On the one-and-twentieth day of April, Domagaia
came to the shore side, accompanied with divers lusty
and strong men, such as we were not wont to see, and
told us that their lord Donnacona would the next day
come and see us, and bring great store of deer's flesh
and other things with him.   The next day he came and
brought a great number of men to Stadacona, to what
end, and for what cause, we knew not, but (as the
proverb saith) he that takes heed and shields himself
from all men, may hap to scape from some.   For
we had need to look about us, considering how in
number we were diminished, and in strength greatly
weakened, both by reason of our sickness and also
of the number that were dead, so that we were constrained to leave one of our ships in the port of the
Holy Cross.

Our captain was warned of their coming, and how
they had brought a great number of men with them,
for Domagaia came to tell it us, and durst not pass
the river that was betwixt Stadacona and us, as he
was wont to do, whereupon we mistrusted some treason.
Our captain seeing this, sent one of his servants to
them, accompanied with John Poulet, being best
beloved of those people, to see who were there and
what they did.   The said Poulet and the other feigned

themselves only to be come to visit Donnacona, and bring him certain presents, because they had been together a good while in the said Donnacona's town. So soon as he heard of their coming, he got himself to bed, feigning to be very sick. That done, they went to Taignoagny his house to see him, and wheresoever they went they saw so many people, that in a manner one could not stir for another, and such men as they were never wont to see. Taignoagny would not permit our men to enter into any other houses, but still kept them company, and brought them half way to their ships, and told them that if it would please our captain to show him so much favour as to take a lord of the country, whose name was Agonna, of whom he had received some displeasure, and carry him with him into France, he should therefore for ever be bound unto him, and would do for him whatsoever he would command him, and bade the servant come again the next day and bring an answer. Our captain being advertised of so many people that were there, not knowing to what end, purposed to play a pretty prank, that is to say, to take their lord Donnacona, Taignoagny, Domagaia, and some more of the chiefest of them prisoners, insomuch as before he had purposed, to bring them into France, to show unto our king what he had seen in those western parts, and marvels of the world ; for that Donnacona had told us that he had been in the country of Saguenay, in which are infinite rubies, gold, and other riches, and that there are white men, who clothe themselves with woollen cloth even as we do in France. Moreover, he reported that he had been in another country of a people called Picquemians, and other strange people. The said lord was an old man, and even from his childhood had never left off nor ceased from travelling into strange countries, as well by water and rivers as by land.

The said Poulet and the other having told our captain their embassage, and showed him what Taignoagny his will was, the next day he sent his servant again to bid Taignoagny come and see him, and show what he should, for he should be very well entertained, and also part of his will should be accomplished. Taignoagny sent him word that the next day he would come and bring the lord Donnacona with him, and him that had so offended him. Which he did not, but stayed two days; in which time none came from Stadacona to our ships as they were wont to do, but rather fled from us, as if we would have slain them; so that then we plainly perceived their knavery.

But because they understood that those of Sidatin did frequent our company, and that we had forsaken the bottom of a ship which we would leave, to have the old nails out of it the third day following they came from Stadacona, and most of them without difficulty did pass from one side of the river to the other with small skiffs: but Donnacona would not come over. Taignoagny and Domagaia stood talking together above an hour before they would come over; at last they came to speak with our captain. There Taignoagny prayed him that he would cause the foresaid man to be taken and carried into France. Our captain refused to do it, saying that his king had forbidden him to bring any man or woman into France, only that he might bring two or three young boys to learn the language; but that he would willingly carry him to Newfoundland, and there leave him in an

island. Our captain spake this only to assure them,
that they should bring Donnacona with them, whom
they had left on the other side. Which words, when
Taignoagny heard, he was very glad, thinking he
should never return into France again; and therefore
promised to come the next day, which was the day
of the Holy Cross, and to bring Donnacona and all
the people with him.

Chapter 18

How that upon Holyrood Day our captain caused a
    cross to be set up in our fort: and how the lord
    Donnacona, Taignoagny, Domagaia, and others of
    their company came: and of the taking of the
    said lord.

The third of May, being Holyrood Day, our captain,
for the solemnity of the day, caused a goodly fair cross
of thirty-five foot in height to be set up, under the
crosset of which he caused a shield to be hanged,
wherein were the arms of France, and over them was
written in antique letters, *Franciscus primus Dei gratia
Francorum Rex regnat.*

And upon that day about noon, there came a great
number of the people of Stadacona, men, women, and
children, who told us that their lord Donnacona,
Taignoagny, and Domagaia were coming, whereof we
were very glad, hoping to retain them. About two
of the clock in the afternoon they came, and being
come near our ships, our captain went to salute Donnacona, who also showed him a merry countenance,
albeit very fearfully his eyes were still bent toward
the wood. Shortly after came Taignoagny, who bade

Donnacona that he should not enter into our fort, and therefore fire was brought forth by one of our men, and kindled where their lord was. Our captain prayed him to come into our ships to eat and drink as he was wont to do, and also Taignoagny, who promised that after a while he would come; and so they did, and entered into our ships. But first it was told our captain by Domagaia that Taignoagny had spoken ill of him, and that he had bid Donnacona he should not come aboard our ships. Our captain perceiving that, came out of the fort, and saw that only by Taignoagny his warning the women ran away, and none but men stayed in great number, wherefore he straight commanded his men to lay hold on Donnacona, Taignoagny, and Domagaia, and two more of the chiefest whom he pointed unto. Then he commanded them to make the others to retire. Presently after, the said lord entered into the fort with the captain, but by and by Taignoagny came to make him come out again. Our captain, seeing that there was no other remedy, began to call unto them to take them, at whose cry and voice all his men came forth, and took the said lord with the others whom they had appointed to take. The Canadians, seeing their lord taken, began to run away, even as sheep before the wolf, some crossing over the river, some through the woods, each one seeking for his own advantage. That done, we retired ourselves, and laid up the prisoners under good guard and safety.

CHAPTER 19

How the said Canadians the night following came
before our ships to seek their men, crying and
howling all night like wolves: of the talk and
conclusion they agreed upon the next day: and
of the gifts which they gave our captain.

The night following they came before our ships
(the river being betwixt us), striking their breasts,
and crying and howling like wolves, still calling Agouhanna, thinking to speak with him.   Which our captain
for that time would not permit; neither all the next
day till noon, whereupon they made signs unto us that
we had hanged or killed him.   About noon there came
as great a number in a cluster as ever we saw, who
went to hide themselves in the forest, except some,
who with a loud voice would call and cry to Donnacona
to speak unto them.   Our captain then commanded
Donnacona to be brought up on high to speak unto
them, and bade him be merry, for after he had spoken
and showed unto the King of France what he had seen
in Saguenay and other countries, after ten or twelve
months, he should return again, and that the King
of France would give him great rewards.   Whereat
Donnacona was very glad, and speaking to the others
told it them, who in token of joy gave out three great
cries; and then Donnacona and his people had great
talk together, which for want of interpreters cannot
be described.

Our captain bade Donnacona that he should cause
them to come to the other side of the river, to the end
they might better talk together without any fear, and

that he should assure them. Which Donnacona did, and there came a boat full of the chiefest of them to the ships, and there anew began to talk together, giving great praise to our captain; and gave him a present of four-and-twenty chains of *esurgny*, for that is the greatest and preciousest riches they have in this world, for they esteem more of that than of any gold or silver. After they had long talked together, and that their lord saw that there was no remedy to avoid his going into France, he commanded his people the next day to bring him some victuals to serve him by the way.

Our captain gave Donnacona, as a great present, two frying-pans of copper, eight hatchets, and other small trifles, as knives and beads, whereof he seemed to be very glad, who sent them to his wives and children. Likewise he gave to them that came to speak with Donnacona: they thanked him greatly for them, and then went to their lodgings.

CHAPTER 20

How the next day, being the fifth of May, the said people came again to speak unto their lord, and how four women came to the shore to bring him victuals.

Upon the fifth of May, very early in the morning, a great number of the said people came again to speak unto their lord, and sent a boat, which in their tongue they call *casnoni*, wherein were only four women, without any man, for fear their men should be retained. These women brought great store of victuals, as great millet (which is their corn that they live withal), flesh, fish, and other things after their fashion.

The women being come to our ships, our captain did very friendly entertain them. Then Donnacona prayed our captain to tell those women that he should come again after ten or twelve months, and bring Donnacona to Canada with him: this he said only to appease them. Which our captain did: wherefore the women, as well by words as signs, seemed to be very glad, giving our captain thanks, and told him if he came again, and brought Donnacona with him, they would give him many things. In sign whereof each one gave our captain a chain of *esurgny*, and then passed to the other side of the river again, where stood all the people of Stadacona, who taking all leave of their lord went home again.

On Saturday following, being the sixth of the month, we departed out of the said port of St Croix, and came to harbour a little beneath the Island of Orleans, about twelve leagues from the port of the Holy Cross: and upon Sunday we came to the Island of Filberts, where we stayed until the sixteenth of that month, till the fierceness of the waters were past, which at that time ran too swift a course, and were too dangerous to come down along the river, and therefore we stayed till fair weather came.

In the meanwhile, many of Donnacona's subjects came from the river of Saguenay to him, but being by Domagaia advertised that their lord was taken to be carried into France, they were all amazed. Yet for all that they would not leave to come to our ships to speak to Donnacona, who told them that after twelve months he should come again, and that he was very well used by the captain, gentlemen, and mariners. Which when they heard, they greatly thanked our captain, and gave their lord three bundles of beavers' and sea-wolves' skins, with a great knife of red copper that cometh from Saguenay, and other things. They gave also to our captain a chain of *esurgny*, for which our captain gave them ten or twelve hatchets, and they gave him hearty thanks, and were very well contented.

The next day, being the sixteenth of May, we hoised sail, and came from the said Island of Filberts to another about fifteen leagues from it, which is about five leagues in length; and there, to the end we might take some rest the night following, we stayed that day, in hope the next day we might pass and avoid the dangers of the river of Saguenay, which are great. That evening we went a-land, and found great store of hares, of which we took a great many, and therefore we called it the Island of Hares. In the night there arose a contrary wind, with such storms and tempest, that we were constrained to return to the Island of Filberts again, from whence we were come, because there was none other passage among the said islands, and there we stayed till the one-and-twentieth of that month, till fair weather and good wind came again. And then we sailed again, and that so prosperously, that we passed to Honguedo; which passage until that time had not been discovered. We caused our ships to course athwart Cape Prat, which is the beginning of the Port of Chaleur: and because the wind was good and convenient, we sailed all day and all night without staying, and the next day we came to the middle of Brion's Island, which we were not minded to do, to the end we might shorten our way. These

two lands lie north-west and south-east, and are about
fifty leagues one from another.   The said island is
in latitude 47 degrees and a half.

Upon Thursday, being the twenty-fifth of the month,
and the feast of the Ascension of our Lord, we coasted
over to a land and shallow of low sands, which are
about eight leagues south-west from Brion's Island,
above which are large champaigns full of trees, and
also an enclosed sea, whereas we could neither see
nor perceive any gap or way to enter thereinto.   On
Friday following, being the 26 of the month, because
the wind did change on the coast, we came to Brion's
Island again, where we stayed till the beginning of
June.   And toward the south-east of this island we
saw a land, seeming unto us as an island.   We coasted
it about two leagues and a half, and by the way we
had notice of three other high islands, lying toward
the sands.   After we had known these things, we
returned to the cape of the said land, which doth
divide itself into two or three very high capes: the
waters there are very deep, and the flood of the sea
runneth so swift that it cannot possibly be swifter.
That day we came to Cape Lorraine, which is forty-
seven degrees and a half toward the south.   On which
cape there is a low land, and it seemeth that there is
some entrance of a river, but there is no haven of any
worth.   Above these lands we saw another cape
toward the south.   We named it St Paul's Cape:
it is at 47 degrees and a quarter.

The Sunday following, being the fourth of June,
and Whitsunday, we had notice of the coast lying
east-south-east, distant from the new found land
about two-and-twenty leagues; and because the wind

was against us, we went to a haven, which we named
St Spiritus Port, where we stayed till Tuesday that we
departed thence, sailing along that coast until we came
to St Peter's Islands.   We found along the said coast
many very dangerous islands and shelves, which lie
all in the way east-south-east and west-north-west
about three-and-twenty leagues into the sea.   Whilst
we were in the said St Peter's Islands we met with
many ships of France and of Britain.   We stayed
there from St Barnabas Day, being the eleventh of
the month, until the sixteenth that we departed thence,
and came to Cape Race, and entered into a port called
Rognoso, where we took in fresh water and wood to
pass the sea : there we left one of our boats.

Then upon Monday, being the nineteenth of June,
we went from that port, and with such good and
prosperous weather we sailed along the sea, in such
sort that upon the sixth of July, 1536, we came to the
port of St Malo, by the grace of God, to Whom we pray,
here ending our navigation, that of His infinite mercy
He will grant us His grace and favour, and in the
end bring us to the place of everlasting felicity.   Amen.

Portrait of Sir Humfrey Gilbert

GILBERT'S VOYAGE (1583)

A report of the voyage and success thereof, attempted
in the year of our Lord 1583 by Sir Humfrey
Gilbert, Knight, with other gentlemen assisting
him in that action, intended to discover and to
plant Christian inhabitants in place convenient,
upon those large and ample countries extended
northward from the Cape of Florida, lying under
very temperate climes, esteemed fertile and rich
in minerals, yet not in the actual possession of
any Christian prince. Written by Master Edward
Hayes, gentleman, and principal actor in the same
voyage, who alone continued unto the end, and
by God's special assistance returned home with
his retinue safe and entire.

We began our voyage upon Tuesday, the eleventh
day of June, in the year of our Lord 1583, having in
our fleet (at our departure from Cawset Bay) these
ships, whose names and burthens, with the names of
the captains and masters of them, I have also inserted,
as followeth:

1. The *Delight, alias* the *George,* of burthen 120
tons, was Admiral; in which went the General, and
William Winter, captain in her and part owner, and
Richard Clarke, master. 2. The bark *Ralegh,* set

forth by Master Walter Ralegh, of the burthen of
200 tons, was then Vice-Admiral; in which went
Master Butler, captain, and Robert Davis, of Bristol,
master.   3. The *Golden Hind*, of burthen 40 tons,
was then Rear-Admiral; in which went Edward Hayes,
captain and owner, and William Cox, of Limehouse,
master.   4. The *Swallow*, of burthen 40 tons; in
her was captain Maurice Browne.   5. The *Squirrel*,
of burthen 10 tons; in which went captain William
Andrewes, and one Cade, master.   We were in number
in all about 260 men; among whom we had of every
faculty good choice, as shipwrights, masons, carpenters,
smiths, and such like, requisite to such an action;
also mineral men and refiners.   Besides, for solace of
our people, and allurement of the savages, we were
provided of music in good variety; not omitting the
least toys, as morris dancers, hobby-horse, and May-
like conceits to delight the savage people, whom we
intended to win by all fair means possible.   And to that
end we were indifferently furnished of all petty haber-
dashery wares to barter with those simple people.

In this manner we set forward, departing (as hath
been said) out of Cawset Bay the eleventh day of
June, being Tuesday, the weather and wind fair and
good all day, but a great storm of thunder and wind
fell the same night.   Thursday following, when we
hailed one another in the evening, they signified unto
us out of the Vice-Admiral, that both the captain,
and very many of the men, were fallen sick.   And
about midnight the Vice-Admiral forsook us, notwithstanding we had the wind east, fair and good.   But
it was after credibly reported, that they were infected
with a contagious sickness, and arrived greatly dis-

tressed at Plymouth: the reason I could never understand. Sure I am, no cost was spared by their owner, Master Ralegh, in setting them forth: therefore I leave it unto God. By this time we were in 48 degrees of latitude, not a little grieved with the loss óf the most puissant ship in our fleet; after whose departure, the *Golden Hind* succeeded in the place of Vice-Admiral, and removed her flag from the mizen unto the foretop. From Saturday, the 15 of June, until the 28, which was upon a Friday, we never had fair day without fog or rain, and winds bad, much to the west-north-west, whereby we were driven southward unto 41 degrees scarce.

About this time of the year the winds are commonly west towards the Newfoundland, keeping ordinarily within two points of west to the south or to the north, whereby the course thither falleth out to be long and tedious after June, which in March, April, and May, hath been performed out of England in 22 days and less. We had wind always so scant from west-north-west, and from west-south-west again, that our traverse was great, running south unto 41 degrees almost, and afterward north into 51 degrees. Also we were encumbered with much fog and mists in manner palpable, in which we could not keep so well together, but were dissevered, losing the company of the *Swallow* and the *Squirrel* upon the 20 day of July, whom we met again at several places upon the Newfoundland coast the third of August, as shall be declared in place convenient. Saturday, the 27 of July, we might descry, not far from us, as it were mountains of ice driven upon the sea, being then in 50 degrees, which were carried southward to the weather of us: whereby may be conjectured that some current doth set that way from the north.

Before we come to Newfoundland, about 50 leagues on this side, we pass the bank, which are high grounds rising within the sea and under water, yet deep enough and without danger, being commonly not less than 25 and 30 fathom water upon them: the same (as it were some vein of mountains within the sea) do run along and from the Newfoundland, beginning northward about 52 or 53 degrees of latitude, and do extend into the south infinitely. The breadth of this bank is somewhere more, and somewhere less; but we found the same about 10 leagues over, having sounded both on this side thereof, and the other toward Newfoundland, but found no ground with almost 200 fathom of line, both before and after we had passed the bank. The Portugals, and French chiefly, have a notable trade of fishing upon this bank, where are sometimes an hundred or more sails of ships; who commonly begin the fishing in April, and have ended by July. That fish is large, always wet, having no land near to dry, and is called cod fish. During the time of fishing, a man shall know without sounding when he is upon the bank, by the incredible multitude of sea-fowl hovering over the same, to prey upon the offals and garbage of fish thrown out by fishermen, and floating upon the sea.

Upon Tuesday, the 11 of June, we forsook the coast of England. So again Tuesday, the 30 of July, seven weeks after, we got sight of land, being immediately embayed in the Grand Bay, or some other great bay; the certainty whereof we could not judge, so great haze and fog did hang upon the coast, as neither we might discern the land well, nor take the sun's height. But by our best computation we were then in the 51 degrees of latitude.

Forsaking this bay and uncomfortable coast (nothing appearing unto us but hideous rocks and mountains, bare of trees, and void of any green herb) we followed the coast to the south, with weather fair and clear. We had sight of an island named Penguin, of a fowl there breeding in abundance almost incredible, which cannot fly, their wings not able to carry their body, being very large (not much less than a goose) and exceeding fat, which the Frenchmen use to take without difficulty upon that island, and to barrel them up with salt. But for lingering of time, we had made us there the like provision.

Trending this coast, we came to the island called Baccalaos, being not past two leagues from the main: to the south thereof lieth Cape St Francis, 5 leagues distant from Baccalaos, between which goeth in a great bay, by the vulgar sort called the Bay of Conception. Here we met with the *Swallow* again, whom we had lost in the fog, and all her men altered into other apparel; whereof it seemed their store was so amended, that for joy and congratulation of our meeting, they spared not to cast up into the air and overboard their caps and hats in good plenty. The captain, albeit himself was very honest and religious, yet was he not appointed of men to his humour and desert; who for the most part were such as had been by us surprised upon the narrow seas of England, being pirates, and had taken at that instant certain Frenchmen laden, one bark with wines, and another with salt. Both which we rescued, and took the man-of-

war with all her men, which was the same ship now
called the *Swallow*: following still their kind so oft
as, being separated from the General, they found
opportunity to rob and spoil. And because God's
justice did follow the same company, even to destruc-
tion, and to the overthrow also of the captain (though
not consenting to their misdemeanour) I will not
conceal anything that maketh to the manifestation
and approbation of His judgments, for examples of
others; persuaded that God more sharply took revenge
upon them, and hath tolerated longer as great outrage
in others, by how much these went under protection
of His cause and religion, which was then pretended.

Therefore upon further enquiry it was known, how
this company met with a bark returning home after
the fishing with his freight; and because the men in
the *Swallow* were very near scanted of victual, and
chiefly of apparel, doubtful withal where or when to
find and meet with their Admiral, they besought the
captain they might go aboard this Newlander, only
to borrow what might be spared, the rather because
the same was bound homeward. Leave given, not
without charge to deal favourably, they came aboard
the fisherman, whom they rifled of tackle, sails, cables,
victuals, and the men of their apparel: not sparing
by torture, winding cords about their heads, to draw
out else what they thought good. This done with
expedition, like men skilful in such mischief, as they
took their cock-boat to go aboard their own ship, it
was overwhelmed in the sea, and certain of these men
there drowned: the rest were preserved even by those
silly souls whom they had before spoiled, who saved
and delivered them aboard the *Swallow*. What became

afterward of the poor Newlander, perhaps destitute of sails and furniture sufficient to carry them home, whither they had not less to run than 700 leagues, God alone knoweth, who took vengeance not long after of the rest that escaped at this instant, to reveal the fact, and justify to the world God's judgments inflicted upon them, as shall be declared in place convenient.

Thus after we had met with the *Swallow*, we held on our course southward, until we came against the harbour called St John, about 5 leagues from the former Cape of St Francis; where before the entrance into the harbour, we found also the frigate or *Squirrel* lying at anchor; whom the English merchants, that were and always be Admirals by turns interchangeably over the fleets of fishermen within the same harbour, would not permit to enter into the harbour. Glad of so happy meeting, both of the *Swallow* and frigate in one day, being Saturday, the 3 of August, we made ready our fights, and prepared to enter the harbour, any resistance to the contrary notwithstanding, there being within of all nations to the number of 36 sails. But first the General dispatched a boat to give them knowledge of his coming for no ill intent, having commission from her Majesty for his voyage he had in hand. And immediately we followed with a slack gale, and in the very entrance, which is but narrow, not above 2 butts' length, the Admiral fell upon a rock on the larboard side by great oversight, in that the weather was fair, the rock much above water fast by the shore, where neither went any sea-gate. But we found such readiness in the English merchants to help us in that danger, that without delay there were brought a number of boats, which towed off the ship, and cleared her of danger.

Having taken place convenient in the road, we let fall anchors, the captains and masters repairing aboard our Admiral: whither also came immediately the masters and owners of the fishing fleet of Englishmen, to understand the General's intent and cause of our arrival there. They were all satisfied when the General had shewed his commission, and purpose to take possession of those lands to the behalf of the crown of England, and the advancement of Christian religion in those paganish regions, requiring but their lawful aid for repairing of his fleet, and supply of some necessaries, so far as conveniently might be afforded him, both out of that and other harbours adjoining. In lieu whereof, he made offer to gratify them with any favour and privilege, which upon their better advice they should demand, the like being not to be obtained hereafter for greater price. So craving expedition of his demand, minding to proceed further south without long detention in those parts, he dismissed them, after promise given of their best endeavour to satisfy speedily his so reasonable request. The merchants with their masters departed, they caused forthwith to be discharged all the great ordnance of their fleet in token of our welcome.

It was further determined that every ship of our fleet should deliver unto the merchants and masters of that harbour a note of all their wants: which done, the ships, as well English as strangers, were taxed at an easy rate to make supply. And besides, commissioners were appointed, part of our own company and part of theirs, to go into other harbours adjoining

(for our English merchants command all there) to levy
our provision: whereunto the Portugals, above other
nations, did most willingly and liberally contribute.
Insomuch as we were presented (above our allowance)
with wines, marmalades, most fine rusk or biscuit, sweet
oils, and sundry delicacies. Also we wanted not of fresh
salmons, trouts, lobsters, and other fresh fish brought
daily unto us. Moreover as the manner is in their
fishing, every week to choose their Admiral anew,
or rather they succeed in orderly course, and have
weekly their Admiral's feast solemnized: even so the
General, captains, and masters of our fleet were continually invited and feasted. To grow short, in our
abundance at home the entertainment had been
delightful; but after our wants and tedious passage
through the ocean, it seemed more acceptable and of
greater contentation, by how much the same was
unexpected in that desolate corner of the world; where,
at other times of the year, wild beasts and birds have
only the fruition of all those countries, which now
seemed a place very populous and much frequented.

The next morning being Sunday and the 4 of
August, the General and his company were brought
on land by English merchants, who shewed unto us
their accustomed walks unto a place they call the
Garden. But nothing appeared more than nature
itself without art; who confusedly hath brought forth
roses abundantly, wild, but odoriferous, and to sense
very comfortable. Also the like plenty of raspis
berries, which do grow in every place.

Monday following, the General had his tent set up,
who being accompanied with his own followers, sum-
moned the merchants and masters, both English and

strangers, to be present at his taking possession of those countries. Before whom openly was read, and interpreted unto the strangers, his commission: by virtue whereof he took possession, in the same harbour of St John, and 200 leagues every way, invested the Queen's Majesty with the title and dignity thereof, had delivered unto him (after the custom of England) a rod, and a turf of the same soil, entering possession also for him, his heirs and assigns for ever; and signified unto all men, that from that time forward, they should take the same land as a territory appertaining to the Queen of England, and himself authorised under her Majesty to possess and enjoy it, and to ordain laws for the government thereof, agreeable, so near as conveniently might be, unto the laws of England, under which all people coming thither hereafter, either to inhabit, or by way of traffic, should be subjected and governed. And especially at the same time for a beginning, he proposed and delivered three laws to be in force immediately. That is to say: the first for religion, which in public exercise should be according to the Church of England. The second, for maintenance of her Majesty's right and possession of those territories, against which if anything were attempted prejudicial, the party or parties offending should be adjudged and executed as in case of high treason, according to the laws of England. The third, if any person should utter words sounding to the dishonour of her Majesty, he should lose his ears, and have his ship and goods confiscate.

These contents published, obedience was promised by general voice and consent of the multitude, as well of Englishmen as strangers, praying for continuance of this possession and government begun. After this, the assembly was dismissed. And afterward were erected not far from that place the arms of England engraven in lead, and infixed upon a pillar of wood. Yet further and actually to establish this possession taken in the right of her Majesty, and to the behoof of Sir Humfrey Gilbert, Knight, his heirs and assigns for ever, the General granted in fee farm divers parcels of land lying by the water-side, both in this harbour of St John, and elsewhere, which was to the owners a great commodity, being thereby assured, by their proper inheritance, of grounds convenient to dress and to dry their fish; whereof many times before they did fail, being prevented by them that came first into the harbour. For which grounds they did covenant to pay a certain rent and service unto Sir Humfrey Gilbert, his heirs or assigns for ever, and yearly to maintain possession of the same, by themselves or their assigns.

Now remained only to take in provision granted, according as every ship was taxed, which did fish upon the coast adjoining. In the meanwhile, the General appointed men unto their charge: some to repair and trim the ships, others to attend in gathering together our supply and provisions: others to search the commodities and singularities of the country, to be found by sea or land, and to make relation unto the General what either themselves could know by their own travail and experience, or by good intelligence of Englishmen or strangers, who had longest frequented the same coast. Also some observed the elevation of the pole, and drew plots of the country exactly graded. And by that I could gather by each man's several relation, I have drawn a brief description of the Newfoundland, with the commodities by sea or land already made, and such also as are in possibility and great likelihood to be made. Nevertheless the cards and plots that were drawn, with the due gradation of the harbours, bays, and capes, did perish with the Admiral: wherefore in the description following, I must omit the particulars of such things.

That which we do call the Newfoundland, and the Frenchmen Baccalaos, is an island, or rather (after the opinion of some) it consisteth of sundry islands and broken lands, situate in the north regions of America, upon the gulf and entrance of the great river called St Lawrence in Canada. Into the which, navigation may be made both on the south and north side of this island. The land lieth south and north, containing in length between 300 and 400 miles, accounting from Cape Race, which is in 46 degrees 25 minutes, unto the Grand Bay in 52 degrees of septentrional latitude. The island round about hath very many goodly bays and harbours, safe roads for ships, the like not to be found in any part of the known world.

In the south parts we found no inhabitants, which by all likelihood have abandoned those coasts, the same being so much frequented by Christians; but in the north are savages altogether harmless. Touching the commodities of this country, serving either for sustentation of inhabitants, or for maintenance of traffic, there are and may be made divers; so that it seemeth nature hath recompensed that only defect and incommodity of some sharp cold, by many benefits: namely, with incredible quantity, and no less variety of kinds of fish in the sea and fresh waters, as trouts, salmons, and other fish to us unknown; also cod, which alone draweth many nations thither, and is become the most famous fishing of the world; abundance of whales, for which also is a very great trade in the bays of Placentia and the Grand Bay, where is made train oil of the whale; herring, the largest that have been heard of, and exceeding the Marstrand herring of Norway: but hitherto was never benefit taken of the herring fishing. There are sundry other fish very delicate, namely, the bonito, lobsters, turbot, with others infinite not sought after; oysters having pearl but not orient in colour: I took it, by reason they were not gathered in season.

Concerning the inland commodities, as well to be drawn from this land, as from the exceeding large countries adjoining: there is nothing which our east and northerly countries of Europe do yield, but the like also may be made in them as plentifully, by time and industry: namely, resin, pitch, tar, soap-ashes, deal-board, masts for ships, hides, furs, flax, hemp, corn, cables, cordage, linen cloth, metals, and many more. All which the countries will afford, and the soil is apt to yield. The trees for the most in those south parts are fir-trees, pine, and cypress, all yielding gum and turpentine; cherry trees bearing fruit no bigger than a small pease; also pear trees, but fruitless. Other trees of some sorts to us unknown. The soil along the coast is not deep of earth, bringing forth abundantly peason small, yet good feeding for cattle. Roses passing sweet, like unto our musk roses in form; raspises; a berry which we call whorts, good and wholesome to eat. The grass and herb doth fat sheep in very short space, proved by English merchants which have carried sheep thither for fresh victual and had them raised exceeding fat in less than three weeks. Peason which our countrymen have sown in the time of May, have come up fair, and been gathered in the beginning of August, of which our General had a present acceptable for the rareness, being the first fruits coming up by art and industry in that desolate and dishabited land.

Lakes or pools of fresh water, both on the tops of mountains and in the valleys; in which are said to be mussels not unlike to have pearl, which I had put in trial, if by mischance falling unto me I had not been letted from that and other good experiments I was minded to make. Fowl both of water and land in great plenty and diversity. All kind of green fowl: others as big as bustards, yet not the same. A great white fowl called of some a gaunt. Upon the land divers sorts of hawks, as falcons, and others by report. Partridges most plentiful, larger than ours, gray and white of colour, and rough-footed like doves, which our men after one flight did kill with cudgels, they were so fat and unable to fly. Birds, some like black-birds, linnets, canary birds, and other very small. Beasts of sundry kinds; red deer, buffles, or a beast as it seemeth by the tract and foot very large, in manner of an ox. Bears, ounces or leopards, some greater and some lesser, wolves, foxes, which to the northward a little further are black, whose fur is esteemed in some countries of Europe very rich. Otters, beavers, martens; and in the opinion of most men that saw it, the General had brought unto him a sable alive, which he sent unto his brother, Sir John Gilbert, Knight, of Devonshire: but it was never delivered, as after

I understood. We could not observe the hundredth part of creatures in those unhabited lands: but these mentioned may induce us to glorify the magnificent God, who hath superabundantly replenished the earth with creatures serving for the use of man, though man hath not used a fifth part of the same, which the more doth aggravate the fault and foolish sloth in many of our nation, choosing rather to live indirectly, and very miserably to live and die within this realm pestered with inhabitants, than to adventure as becometh men, to obtain an habitation in those remote lands, in which nature very prodigally doth minister unto men's endeavours, and for art to work upon. For besides these already recounted and infinite more, the mountains generally make shew of mineral sub-stance: iron very common, lead, and somewhere copper. I will not aver of richer metals; albeit by the circumstances following, more than hope may be conceived thereof.

For amongst other charges given to enquire out the singularities of this country, the General was most curious in the search of metals, commanding the mineral-man and refiner especially to be diligent. The same was a Saxon born, honest and religious, named Daniel. Who after search brought at first some sort of ore, seeming rather to be iron than other metal. The next time he found ore, which with no small shew of contentment he delivered unto the General, using protestation, that if silver were the thing which might satisfy the General and his followers, there it was, advising him to seek no further: the peril whereof he undertook upon his life (as dear unto him as the crown of England unto her Majesty, that

I may use his own words) if it fell not out accordingly.

Myself at this instant liker to die than to live, by a mischance, could not follow this confident opinion of our refiner to my own satisfaction; but afterward demanding our General's opinion therein, and to have some part of the ore, he replied: "Content yourself, I have seen enough; and were it but to satisfy my private humour, I would proceed no further. The promise unto my friends, and necessity to bring also the south countries within compass of my patent near expired, as we have already done these north parts, do only persuade me further. And touching the ore, I have sent it aboard, whereof I would have no speech to be made so long as we remain within harbour: here being both Portugals, Biscayans, and Frenchmen, not far off, from whom must be kept any bruit or muttering of such matter. When we are at sea, proof shall be made: if it be to our desire, we may return the sooner hither again." Whose answer I judged reasonable, and contenting me well: wherewith I will conclude this narration and description of the Newfoundland, and proceed to the rest of our voyage, which ended tragically.

While the better sort of us were seriously occupied in repairing our wants, and contriving of matters for the commodity of our voyage, others of another sort and disposition were plotting of mischief; some casting to steal away our shipping by night, watching opportunity by the General's and captains' lying on the shore: whose conspiracies discovered, they were prevented. Others drew together in company, and

carried away out of the harbours adjoining a ship
laden with fish, setting the poor men on shore. A great
many more of our people stole into the woods to hide
themselves, attending time and means to return home
by such shipping as daily departed from the coast.
Some were sick of fluxes, and many dead: and in
brief, by one means or other our company was
diminished, and many by the General licensed to
return home. Insomuch as after we had reviewed
our people, resolved to see an end of our voyage, we
grew scant of men to furnish all our shipping: it
seemed good therefore unto the General to leave the
Swallow with such provision as might be spared for
transporting home the sick people.

The captain of the *Delight*, or Admiral, returned
into England, in whose stead was appointed captain
Maurice Browne, before captain of the *Swallow*; who
also brought with him into the *Delight* all his men of
the *Swallow*, which before have been noted of outrage
perpetrated and committed upon fishermen there met
at sea.

The General made choice to go in his frigate, the
Squirrel, whereof the captain also was amongst them
that returned into England; the same frigate being
most convenient to discover upon the coast, and to
search into every harbour or creek, which a great
ship could not do. Therefore the frigate was prepared
with her nettings and fights, and overcharged with
bases and such small ordnance, more to give a shew,
than with judgment to foresee unto the safety of her
and the men, which afterward was an occasion also
of their overthrow.

Now having made ready our shipping, that is to

say, the *Delight*, the *Golden Hind*, and the *Squirrel*, we put aboard our provision, which was wines, bread or rusk, fish wet and dry, sweet oils; besides many other, as marmalades, figs, lemons barrelled, and such like. Also we had other necessary provisions for trimming our ships, nets and lines to fish withal, boats or pinnaces fit for discovery. In brief, we were supplied of our wants commodiously, as if we had been in a country or some city populous and plentiful of all things.

We departed from this harbour of St John's upon Tuesday, the twentieth of August, which we found by exact observation to be in 47 degrees 40 minutes. And the next day by night we were at Cape Race, 25 leagues from the same harborough. This cape lieth south-south-west from St John's: it is a low land, being off from the cape about half a league: within the sea riseth up a rock against the point of the cape, which thereby is easily known. It is in latitude 46 degrees 25 minutes. Under this cape we were becalmed a small time, during which we laid out hooks and lines to take cod, and drew in less than two hours fish so large and in such abundance, that many days after we fed upon no other provision. From hence we shaped our course unto the Island of Sablon, if conveniently it would so fall out, also directly to Cape Breton.

Sablon lieth to the seaward of Cape Breton about 25 leagues, whither we were determined to go upon intelligence we had of a Portugal, during our abode in St John's, who was himself present when the Portugals (above thirty years past) did put into the same island both neat and swine to breed, which were since

exceedingly multiplied. This seemed unto us very
happy tidings, to have in an island lying so near
unto the main, which we intended to plant upon,
such store of cattle, whereby we might at all times
conveniently be relieved of victual, and served of
store for breed.

In this course we trended along the coast, which
from Cape Race stretcheth into the north-west, making
a bay which some called Trepassa. Then it goeth
out again toward the west, and maketh a point, which
with Cape Race lieth in manner east and west. But
this point inclineth to the north: to the west of which
goeth in the Bay of Placentia. We sent men on land
to take view of the soil along this coast, whereof they
made good report, and some of them had will to be
planted there. They saw pease growing in great
abundance everywhere.

The distance between Cape Race and Cape Breton
is 87 leagues. In which navigation we spent 8 days,
having many times the wind indifferent good; yet
could we never attain sight of any land all that time,
seeing we were hindered by the current. At last we
fell into such flats and dangers, that hardly any of
us escaped: where nevertheless we lost our Admiral
with all the men and provision, not knowing certainly
the place.

Upon Tuesday, the 27 of August, toward the
evening, our General caused them in his frigate to
sound, who found white sand at 35 fathom, being
then in latitude about 44 degrees. Wednesday,
toward night, the wind came south, and we bare with
the land all that night, west-north-west, contrary to
the mind of Master Cox: nevertheless we followed

the Admiral, deprived of power to prevent a mischief, which by no contradiction could be brought to hold other course, alleging they could not make the ship to work better, nor to lie otherways. The evening was fair and pleasant, yet not without token of storm to ensue, and most part of this Wednesday night, like the swan that singeth before her death, they in the Admiral, or *Delight*, continued in sounding of trumpets, with drums and fifes; also winding the cornets and hautboys, and in the end of their jollity, left with the battle and ringing of doleful knells. Towards the evening also we caught in the *Golden Hind* a very mighty porpoise with a harping iron, having first stricken divers of them, and brought away part of their flesh sticking upon the iron, but could recover only that one. These also, passing through the ocean in herds, did portend storm. I omit to recite frivolous reports by them in the frigate, of strange voices the same night, which scared some from the helm.

Thursday, the 29 of August, the wind rose, and blew vehemently at south and by east, bringing withal rain and thick mist, so that we could not see a cable length before us. And betimes in the morning we were altogether run and folded in amongst flats and sands, amongst which we found shoal and deep in every three or four ship's length, after we began to sound: but first we were upon them unawares, until Master Cox looking out, discerned (in his judgment) white cliffs, crying "Land!" withal; though we could not afterward descry any land, it being very likely the breaking of the sea white, which seemed to be white cliffs, through the haze and thick weather.

Immediately tokens were given unto the *Delight*, to cast about to seaward, which, being the greater ship, and of burden 120 tons, was yet foremost upon the breach, keeping so ill watch, that they knew not the danger, before they felt the same, too late to recover it; for presently the Admiral struck aground, and had soon after her stern and hinder parts beaten in pieces. Whereupon the rest (that is to say, the frigate, in which was the General, and the *Golden Hind*) cast about east-south-east, bearing to the south, even for our lives, into the wind's eye, because that way carried us to the seaward. Making out from this danger, we sounded one while seven fathom, then five fathom, then four fathom and less, again deeper, immediately four fathom, then but three fathom, the sea going mightily and high. At last we recovered (God be thanked), in some despair, to sea room enough.

In this distress, we had vigilant eye unto the Admiral, whom we saw cast away, without power to give the men succour, neither could we espy any of the men that leaped overboard to save themselves, either in the same pinnace, or cock, or upon rafters, and such like means presenting themselves to men in those extremities: for we desired to save the men by every possible means. But all in vain, sith God had determined their ruin; yet all that day, and part of the next, we beat up and down as near unto the wreck as was possible for us, looking out if by good hap we might espy any of them.

This was a heavy and grievous event, to lose at one blow our chief ship freighted with great provision, gathered together with much travail, care, long time, and difficulty; but more was the loss of our men, which perished to the number almost of a hundred souls. Amongst whom was drowned a learned man, a Hungarian, born in the city of Buda, called thereof Budæus, who, of piety and zeal to good attempts, adventured in this action, minding to record in the Latin tongue the gests and things worthy of remembrance, happening in this discovery, to the honour of our nation, the same being adorned with the eloquent style of this orator and rare poet of our time.

Here also perished our Saxon refiner and discoverer of inestimable riches, as it was left amongst some of us in undoubted hope. No less heavy was the loss of the captain, Maurice Browne, a virtuous, honest, and discreet gentleman, overseen only in liberty given late before to men, that ought to have been restrained, who shewed himself a man resolved, and never unprepared for death, as by his last act of this tragedy appeared, by report of them that escaped this wreck miraculously, as shall be hereafter declared. For when all hope was past of recovering the ship, and that men began to give over, and to save themselves, the captain was advised before to shift also for his life, by the pinnace at the stern of the ship ; but refusing that counsel, he would not give example with the first to leave the ship, but used all means to exhort his people not to despair, nor so to leave off their labour, choosing rather to die than to incur infamy by forsaking his charge, which then might be thought to have perished through his default, shewing an ill precedent unto his men, by leaving the ship first himself. With this mind he mounted upon the highest deck, where he attended imminent death, and unavoidable :

how long, I leave it to God, who withdraweth not his comfort from his servants at such times.

In the mean season, certain, to the number of fourteen persons, leaped into a small pinnace, the bigness of a Thames barge, which was made in the Newfoundland, cut off the rope wherewith it was towed, and committed themselves to God's mercy, amidst the storm and rage of sea and winds, destitute of food, not so much as a drop of fresh water. The boat seeming overcharged in foul weather with company, Edward Headly, a valiant soldier, and well reputed of his company, preferring the greater to the lesser, thought better that some of them perished than all, made this motion, to cast lots, and them to be thrown overboard upon whom the lots fell, thereby to lighten the boat, which otherways seemed impossible to live, offered himself with the first, content to take his adventure gladly: which nevertheless Richard Clarke, that was master of the Admiral, and one of this number, refused, advising to abide God's pleasure, who was able to save all, as well as a few. The boat was carried before the wind, continuing six days and nights in the ocean, and arrived at last with the men alive, but weak, upon the Newfoundland, saving that the foresaid Headly, who had been late sick, and another called of us Brazil (of his travel into those countries) died by the way, famished, and less able to hold out than those of better health. Thus whom God delivered from drowning, he appointed to be famished; who doth give limits to man's times, and ordaineth the manner and circumstance of dying: whom, again, he will preserve, neither sea nor famine can confound. For those that arrived upon the Newfoundland were brought into France by certain Frenchmen, then being upon that coast.

After this heavy chance, we continued in beating the sea up and down, expecting when the weather would clear up, that we might yet bear in with the land, which we judged not far off, either the continent or some island. For we many times, and in sundry places found ground at 50, 45, 40 fathoms, and less. The ground coming upon our lead, being sometimes oozy sand, and otherwhile a broad shell, with a little sand about it.

Our people lost courage daily after this ill success, the weather continuing thick and blustering, with increase of cold, winter drawing on, which took from them all hope of amendment, settling an assurance of worse weather to grow upon us every day. The leeside of us lay full of flats and dangers inevitable, if the wind blew hard at south. Some again doubted we were ingulfed in the Bay of St Lawrence, the coast full of dangers, and unto us unknown. But above all, provision waxed scant, and hope of supply was gone with loss of our Admiral. Those in the frigate were already pinched with spare allowance, and want of clothes chiefly: whereupon they besought the General to return for England, before they all perished. And to them of the *Golden Hind* they made signs of their distress, pointing to their mouths, and to their clothes thin and ragged: then immediately they also of the *Golden Hind* grew to be of the same opinion and desire to return home.

The former reasons having also moved the General to have compassion of his poor men, in whom he saw no want of good will, but of means fit to perform the action they came for, he resolved upon retire: and calling the captain and master of the *Hind*, he yielded them many reasons, enforcing this unexpected return, withal protesting himself greatly satisfied with that he had seen and knew already, reiterating these words: "Be content, we have seen enough, and take no care of expense past: I will set you forth royally the next spring, if God send us safe home. Therefore I pray you let us no longer strive here, where we fight against the elements." Omitting circumstance, how unwillingly the captain and master of the *Hind* condescended to this motion, his own company can testify; yet comforted with the General's promises of a speedy return at spring, and induced by other apparent reasons, proving an impossibility to accomplish the action at that time, it was concluded on all hands to retire.

So upon Saturday in the afternoon, the 31 of August, we changed our course, and returned back for England. At which very instant, even in winding about, there passed along between us and towards the land which we now forsook a very lion to our seeming, in shape, hair, and colour, not swimming after the manner of a beast by moving of his feet, but rather sliding upon the water with his whole body excepting the legs in sight, neither yet diving under, and again rising above the water, as the manner is of whales, dolphins, tunnies, porpoises, and all other fish: but confidently shewing himself above water without hiding; notwithstanding, we presented ourselves in open view and gesture to amaze him, as all creatures will be commonly at a sudden gaze and sight of men. Thus he passed along turning his head to and fro, yawning and gaping wide, with ugly demonstration of long teeth, and glaring eyes; and to bid us a farewell, coming right against the *Hind* he sent forth a horrible voice, roaring or bellowing as doth a lion, which spectacle we all beheld so far as we were able to discern the same, as men prone to wonder at every strange thing, as this doubtless was, to see a lion in the ocean sea, or fish in shape of a lion. What opinion others had thereof, and chiefly the General himself, I forbear to deliver: but he took it for *bonum omen*, rejoicing that he was to war against such an enemy, if it were the devil. The wind was large for England at our return, but very high, and the sea rough, insomuch as the frigate, wherein the General went, was almost swallowed up.

Monday in the afternoon we passed in the sight of Cape Race, having made as much way in little more than two days and nights back again, as before we had done in eight days from Cape Race unto the place where our ship perished. Which hindrance thitherward, and speed back again, is to be imputed unto the swift current, as well as to the winds, which we had more large in our return. This Monday the General came aboard the *Hind*, to have the surgeon of the *Hind* to dress his foot, which he hurt by treading upon a nail: at what time we comforted each other with hope of hard success to be all past, and of the good to come. So agreeing to carry out lights always by night, that we might keep together, he departed into his frigate, being by no means to be entreated to tarry in the *Hind*, which had been more for his security. Immediately after followed a sharp storm, which we overpassed for that time, praised be God.

The weather fair, the General came aboard the *Hind* again, to make merry together with the captain,

master, and company, which was the last meeting,
and continued there from morning until night. During
which time there passed sundry discourses touching
affairs past and to come, lamenting greatly the loss
of his great ship, more of the men, but most of all of
his books and notes, and what else I know not, for
which he was out of measure grieved, the same doubtless
being some matter of more importance than his books,
which I could not draw from him : yet by circumstance
I gathered the same to be the ore which Daniel the
Saxon had brought unto him in the Newfoundland.
Whatsoever it was, the remembrance touched him so
deep as, not able to contain himself, he beat his boy
in great rage, even at the same time, so long after the
miscarrying of the great ship, because upon a fair day,
when we were becalmed upon the coast of the New
foundland, near unto Cape Race, he sent his boy
aboard the Admiral to fetch certain things : amongst
which, this being chief, was yet forgotten and left
behind. After which time he could never conveniently
send again aboard the great ship, much less he doubted
her ruin so near at hand.

Herein my opinion was better confirmed diversely,
and by sundry conjectures, which maketh me have the
greater hope of this rich mine. For whereas the
General had never before good conceit of these north
parts of the world, now his mind was wholly fixed
upon the Newfoundland. And as before he refused
not to grant assignments liberally to them that required
the same into these north parts, now he became con-
trarily affected, refusing to make any so large grants,
especially of St John's, which certain English merchants
made suit for, offering to employ their money and

travail upon the same: yet neither by their own suit, nor of others of his own company, whom he seemed willing to pleasure, it could be obtained. Also laying down his determination in the spring following for disposing of his voyage then to be re-attempted: he assigned the captain and master of the *Golden Hind* unto the south discovery, and reserved unto himself the north, affirming that this voyage had won his heart from the south, and that he was now become a northern man altogether.

Last, being demanded what means he had, at his arrival in England, to compass the charges of so great preparation as he intended to make the next spring, having determined upon two fleets, one for the south, another for the north: "Leave that to me," he replied, "I will ask a penny of no man. I will bring good tidings unto her Majesty, who will be so gracious to lend me £10,000": willing us therefore to be of good cheer; for he did thank God, he said, with all his heart for that he had seen, the same being enough for us all, and that we needed not to seek any further. And these last words he would often repeat, with demonstration of great fervency of mind, being himself very confident and settled in belief of inestimable good by this voyage: which the greater number of his followers nevertheless mistrusted altogether, not being made partakers of those secrets, which the General kept unto himself. Yet all of them that are living may be witnesses of his words and protestations, which sparingly I have delivered.

Leaving the issue of this good hope unto God, who knoweth the truth only, and can at His good pleasure bring the same to light, I will hasten to the end of this tragedy, which must be knit up in the person of our General. And as it was God's ordinance upon him, even so the vehement persuasion and entreaty of his friends could nothing avail to divert him from a wilful resolution of going through in his frigate, which was overcharged upon their decks with fights, nettings, and small artillery, too cumbersome for so small a boat, that was to pass through the ocean sea at that season of the year, when by course we might expect much storm of foul weather: whereof, indeed, we had enough.

But when he was entreated by the captain, master, and other his well-willers of the *Hind* not to venture in the frigate, this was his answer: "I will not forsake my little company going homeward, with whom I have passed so many storms and perils." And in very truth he was urged to be so over hard, by hard reports given of him that he was afraid of the sea; albeit this was rather rashness than advised resolution, to prefer the wind of a vain report to the weight of his own life. Seeing he would not bend to reason, he had provision out of the *Hind*, such as was wanting aboard his frigate. And so we committed him to God's protection, and set him aboard his pinnace, we being more than 300 leagues onward of our way home.

By that time we had brought the Islands of Azores south of us; yet we then keeping much to the north, until we had got into the height and elevation of England, we met with very foul weather and terrible seas, breaking short and high, pyramid-wise. The reason whereof seemed to proceed either of hilly grounds high and low within the sea, as we see hills and dales upon the land, upon which the seas do mount and fall, or else the cause proceedeth of diversity of winds,

Sir Walter Ralegh

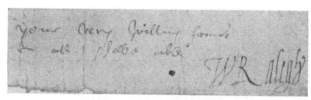

Signature of Sir Walter Ralegh

shifting often in sundry points, all which having power to move the great ocean, which again is not presently settled, so many seas do encounter together, as there had been diversity of winds. Howsoever it cometh to pass, men which all their lifetime had occupied the sea never saw more outrageous seas. We had also upon our mainyard an apparition of a little fire by night, which seamen do call Castor and Pollux. But we had only one, which they take an evil sign of more tempest: the same is usual in storms.

Monday, the ninth of September, in the afternoon, the frigate was near cast away, oppressed by waves, yet at that time recovered; and giving forth signs of joy, the General, sitting abaft with a book in his hand, cried out unto us in the *Hind*, so oft as we did approach within hearing, "We are as near to heaven by sea as by land!" Reiterating the same speech, well beseeming a soldier, resolute in Jesus Christ, as I can testify he was.

The same Monday night, about twelve of the clock, or not long after, the frigate being ahead of us in the *Golden Hind*, suddenly her lights were out, whereof as it were in a moment we lost the sight, and withal our watch cried the General was cast away, which was too true. For in that moment the frigate was devoured and swallowed up of the sea. Yet still we looked out all that night, and ever after until we arrived upon the coast of England; omitting no small sail at sea, unto which we gave not the tokens, between us agreed upon to have perfect knowledge of each other, if we should at any time be separated.

In great torment of weather and peril of drowning, it pleased God to send safe home the *Golden Hind*, which arrived in Falmouth the 22 day of September.

AMADAS AND BARLOW'S VOYAGE
(1584)

The first voyage made to the coasts of America, with
two barks, wherein were Captains Master Philip
Amadas, and Master Arthur Barlow, who discovered part of the country now called Virginia,
Anno 1584. Written by one of the said captains,
and sent to Sir Walter Ralegh, Knight, at whose
charge and direction the said voyage was set forth.

The 27 day of April, in the year of our redemption
1584, we departed the west of England, with two
barks well furnished with men and victuals, having
received our last and perfect directions by your letters,
confirming the former instructions and commandments
delivered by yourself at our leaving the river of Thames.
And I think it a matter both unnecessary, for the
manifest discovery of the country, as also for tedious-
ness' sake, to remember unto you the diurnal of our
course, sailing thither and returning: only I have
presumed to present unto you this brief discourse,
by which you may judge how profitable this land is
likely to succeed, as well to yourself, by whose direction
and charge, and by whose servants, this our discovery
hath been performed, as also to her Highness and the
commonwealth. In which we hope your wisdom
will be satisfied, considering that as much by us hath

been brought to light, as by those small means and number of men we had, could any way have been expected, or hoped for.

The tenth of May we arrived at the Canaries, and the tenth of June in this present year, we were fallen with the islands of the West Indies, keeping a more south-westerly course than was needful, because we doubted that the current of the Bay of Mexico, disboguing between the Cape of Florida and Havana, had been of greater force than afterwards we found it to be. At which islands we found the air very unwholesome, and our men grew for the most part illdisposed: so that having refreshed ourselves with sweet water, and fresh victual, we departed the twelfth day of our arrival there. These islands, with the rest adjoining, are so well known to yourself, and to many others, as I will not trouble you with the remembrance of them.

The second of July we found shoal water, where we smelt so sweet and so strong a smell, as if we had been in the midst of some delicate garden abounding with all kind of odoriferous flowers; by which we were assured that the land could not be far distant. And keeping good watch, and bearing but slack sail, the fourth of the same month we arrived upon the coast, which we supposed to be a continent and firm land, and we sailed along the same a hundred and twenty English miles before we could find any entrance, or river issuing into the sea. The first that appeared unto us we entered, though not without some difficulty, and cast anchor about three arquebus-shot within the haven's mouth, on the left hand of the same; and after thanks given to God for our safe arrival thither, we

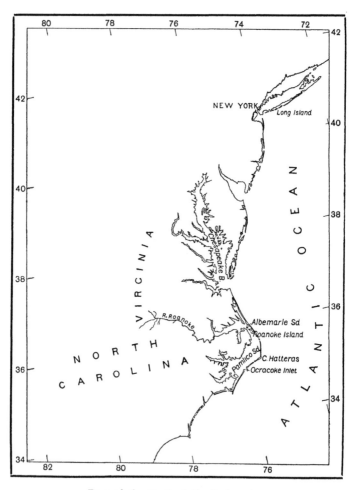

Part of the coast of North America

manned our boats, and went to view the land next adjoining, and to take possession of the same, in the right of the Queen's most excellent Majesty, as rightful queen and princess of the same, and after delivered the same over to your use, according to her Majesty's grant and letters patents, under her Highness' great seal. Which being performed, according to the ceremonies used in such enterprises, we viewed the land about us, being, whereas we first landed, very sandy and low towards the water's side, but so full of grapes as the very beating and surge of the sea overflowed them. Of which we found such plenty, as well there as in all places else, both on the sand and on the green soil on the hills, as in the plains, as well on every little shrub, as also climbing towards the tops of high cedars, that I think in all the world the like abundance is not to be found: and myself having seen those parts of Europe that most abound, find such difference as were incredible to be written.

We passed from the sea side towards the tops of those hills next adjoining, being but of mean height, and from thence we beheld the sea on both sides, to the north and to the south, finding no end any of both ways. This land lay stretching itself to the west, which after we found to be but an island of twenty miles long, and not above six miles broad. Under the bank or hill whereon we stood, we beheld the valleys replenished with goodly cedar trees, and having discharged our arquebus-shot, such a flock of cranes (the most part white) arose under us, with such a cry redoubled by many echoes, as if an army of men had shouted all together.

This island had many goodly woods full of deer,

coneys, hares, and fowl, even in the midst of summer
in incredible abundance. The woods are not such as
you find in Bohemia, Moscovia, or Hercynia, barren
and fruitless, but the highest and reddest cedars of
the world, far bettering the cedars of the Azores, of
the Indies, or Libanus, pines, cypress, sassafras, the
lentisk, or the tree that beareth the mastick; the
tree that beareth the rind of black cinnamon, of which
Master Winter brought from the Straits of Magellan;
and many other of excellent smell and quality. We
remained by the side of this island two whole days
before we saw any people of the country. The third
day we espied one small boat rowing towards us,
having in it three persons. This boat came to the
island side, four arquebus-shot from our ships, and
there two of the people remaining, the third came
along the shore side towards us, and we being then
all within board, he walked up and down upon the
point of the land next unto us. Then the master and
the pilot of the Admiral, Simon Ferdinando, and the
captain Philip Amadas, myself, and others rowed to
the land; whose coming this fellow attended, never
making any shew of fear or doubt. And after he had
spoken of many things not understood by us, we brought
him with his own good liking aboard the ships, and
gave him a shirt, a hat and some other things, and
made him taste of our wine and our meat, which he
liked very well; and after having viewed both barks,
he departed, and went to his own boat again, which he
had left in a little cove or creek adjoining. As soon
as he was two bow-shot into the water, he fell to
fishing, and in less than half an hour he had laden his
boat as deep as it could swim, with which he came

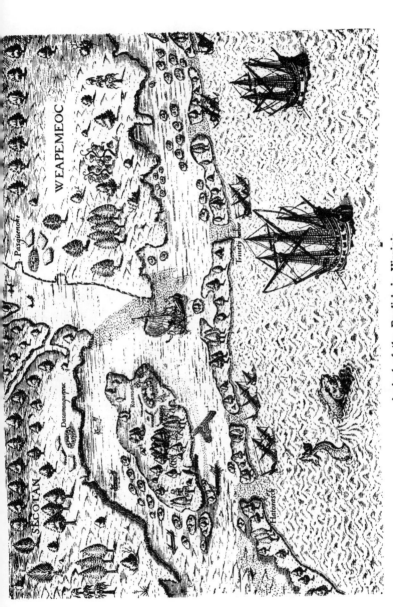

Arrival of the English in Virginia

again to the point of the land, and there he divided
his fish into two parts, pointing one part to the ship,
and the other to the pinnace. Which, after he had,
as much as he might, requited the former benefits
received, departed out of our sight.

The next day there came unto us divers boats,
and in one of them the king's brother, accompanied
with forty or fifty men, very handsome and goodly
people, and in their behaviour as mannerly and civil
as any of Europe. His name was Granganimeo, and
the king is called Wingina, the country Wingandacoa,
and now by her Majesty Virginia. The manner of
his coming was in this sort: he left his boats, altogether
as the first man did, a little from the ships by the
shore, and came along to the place over against the
ships, followed with forty men. When he came to
the place, his servants spread a long mat upon the
ground, on which he sat down, and at the other end
of the mat four others of his company did the like;
the rest of his men stood round about him somewhat
afar off. When we came to the shore to him with our
weapons, he never moved from his place, nor any of
the other four, nor never mistrusted any harm to be
offered from us; but sitting still he beckoned us to
come and sit by him, which we performed; and being
set he made all signs of joy and welcome, striking on
his head and his breast and afterwards on ours, to
shew we were all one, smiling and making shew the
best he could of all love and familiarity. After he
had made a long speech unto us, we presented him
with divers things, which he received very joyfully
and thankfully. None of the company durst speak
one word all the time: only the four which were at

the other end spake one in the other's ear very
softly.

The king is greatly obeyed, and his brothers and
children reverenced. The king himself in person was
at our being there sore wounded in a fight which he
had with the king of the next country, called Piemacum,
and was shot in two places through the body, and once
clean through the thigh, but yet he recovered: by
reason whereof, and for that he lay at the chief town
of the country, being six days' journey off, we saw
him not at all.

After we had presented this his brother with such
things as we thought he liked, we likewise gave somewhat to the other that sat with him on the mat: but
presently he arose and took all from them and put it
into his own basket, making signs and tokens that
all things ought to be delivered unto him, and the
rest were but his servants and followers. A day or
two after this we fell to trading with them, exchanging
some things that we had for chamois, buff, and deer
skins. When we shewed him all our packet of merchandise, of all things that he saw a bright tin dish
most pleased him, which he presently took up and
clapt it before his breast, and after made a hole in the
brim thereof and hung it about his neck, making signs
that it would defend him against his enemies' arrows.
For those people maintain a deadly and terrible war
with the people and king adjoining. We exchanged
our tin dish for twenty skins, worth twenty crowns,
or twenty nobles; and a copper kettle for fifty skins,
worth fifty crowns. They offered us good exchange
for our hatchets and axes, and for knives, and would
have given anything for swords; but we would not

depart with any. After two or three days the king's brother came aboard the ships, and drank wine, and ate of our meat and of our bread, and liked exceedingly thereof. And after a few days overpassed, he brought his wife with him to the ships, his daughter, and two or three children. His wife was very well-favoured, of mean stature, and very bashful. She had on her back a long cloak of leather, with the fur side next to her body, and before her a piece of the same. About her forehead she had a band of white coral, and so had her husband many times. In her ears she had bracelets of pearls hanging down to her middle, whereof we delivered your worship a little bracelet, and those were of the bigness of good pease. The rest of her women of the better sort had pendants of copper hanging in either ear, and some of the children of the king's brother and other noblemen have five or six in either ear: he himself had upon his head a broad plate of gold, or copper; for, being unpolished, we knew not what metal it should be, neither would he by any means suffer us to take it off his head, but feeling it, it would bow very easily. His apparel was as his wife's, only the women wear their hair long on both sides, and the men but on one. They are of colour yellowish, and their hair black for the most part, and yet we saw children that had very fine auburn and chestnut-coloured hair.

After that these women had been there, there came down from all parts great store of people, bringing with them leather, coral, divers kinds of dyes very excellent, and exchanged with us. But when Granganimeo, the king's brother, was present, none durst trade but himself, except such as wear red pieces of copper on their heads like himself; for that is the difference between the noblemen and the governors of countries, and the meaner sort. And we both noted there, and you have understood since by these men which we brought home, that no people in the world carry more respect to their king, nobility, and governors than these do. The king's brother's wife, when she came to us (as she did many times), was followed with forty or fifty women always: and when she came into the ship, she left them all on land, saving her two daughters, her nurse, and one or two more. The king's brother always kept this order: as many boats as he would come withal to the ships, so many fires would he make on the shore afar off, to the end we might understand with what strength and company he approached. Their boats are made of one tree, either of pine, or of pitch-trees; a wood not commonly known to our people, nor found growing in England. They have no edge-tools to make them withal: if they have any they are very few, and those, it seems, they had twenty years since, which, as those two men declared, was out of a wreck which happened upon their coast of some Christian ship, being beaten that way by some storm and outrageous weather, whereof none of the people were saved, but only the ship, or some part of her, being cast upon the sand, out of whose sides they drew the nails and the spikes, and with those they made their best instruments. The manner of making their boats is thus: they burn down some great tree, or take such as are windfallen, and putting gum and resin upon one side thereof, they set fire into it, and when it hath burnt it hollow, they cut out the coal with their shells, and ever where they would burn it deeper or wider they lay on gums, which burn away the timber, and by this means they fashion very fine boats, and such as will transport twenty men. Their oars are like scoops, and many times they set with long poles, as the depth serveth.

The king's brother had great liking of our armour, a sword, and divers other things which we had, and offered to lay a great box of pearl in gage for them: but we refused it for this time, because we would not make them know that we esteemed thereof, until we had understood in what places of the country the pearl grew, which now your worship doth very well understand. He was very just of his promise: for many times we delivered him merchandise upon his word, but ever he came within the day and performed his promise. He sent us every day a brace or two of fat bucks, coneys, hares, fish the best of the world. He sent us divers kinds of fruits, melons, walnuts, cucumbers, gourds, pease, and divers roots, and fruits very excellent good, and of their country corn, which is very white, fair, and well tasted, and groweth three times in five months: in May they sow, in July they reap; in June they sow, in August they reap; in July they sow, in September they reap. Only they cast the corn into the ground, breaking a little of the soft turf with a wooden mattock, or pickaxe. Ourselves proved the soil, and put some of our peas in the ground, and in ten days they were of fourteen inches high. They have also beans very fair of divers colours, and wonderful plenty, some growing naturally, and some in their gardens; and so have they both wheat and oats. The soil is the most plentiful, sweet, fruitful and wholesome of all the world. There are above

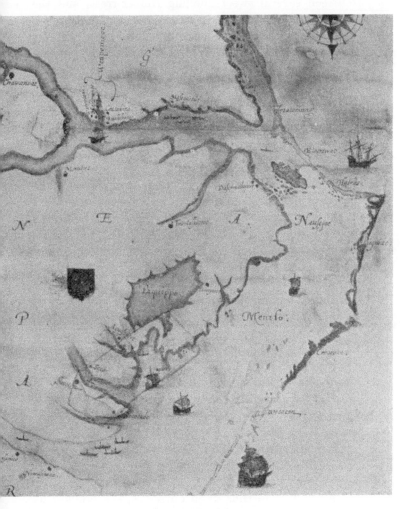

Coast of **Virginia**

fourteen several sweet-smelling timber-trees, and the most part of their underwoods are bays and such like. They have those oaks that we have, but far greater and better. After they had been divers times aboard our ships, myself with seven more went twenty mile into the river that runneth toward the city of Skicoak, which river they call Occam; and the evening following we came to an island which they call Roanoak, distant from the harbour by which we entered seven leagues; and at the north end thereof was a village of nine houses built of cedar, and fortified round about with sharp trees to keep out their enemies, and the entrance into it made like a turnpike very artificially. When we came towards it, standing near unto the water's side, the wife of Granganimeo, the king's brother, came running out to meet us very cheerfully and friendly. Her husband was not then in the village. Some of her people she commanded to draw our boat on shore, for the beating of the billow: others she appointed to carry us on their backs to the dry ground, and others to bring our oars into the house for fear of stealing. When we were come into the utter room (having five rooms in her house), she caused us to sit down by a great fire, and after took off our clothes and washed them, and dried them again. Some of the women plucked off our stockings and washed them, some washed our feet in warm water, and she herself took great pains to see all things ordered in the best manner she could, making great haste to dress some meat for us to eat.

After we had thus dried ourselves, she brought us into the inner room, where she set on the board standing along the house some wheat like furmenty, sodden

The manner of their attire and
painting them selues when
they goe to their generall
huntings or at theire
Solemne feasts.

A native of Virginia

venison, and roasted, fish sodden, boiled, and roasted, melons raw, and sodden, roots of divers kinds, and divers fruits. Their drink is commonly water, but while the grape lasteth they drink wine, and for want of casks to keep it, all the year after they drink water; but it is sodden with ginger in it, and black cinnamon, and sometimes sassafras, and divers other wholesome and medicinable herbs and trees. We were entertained with all love and kindness, and with as much bounty (after their manner) as they could possibly devise. We found the people most gentle, loving, and faithful, void of all guile and treason, and such as live after the manner of the golden age. The people only care how to defend themselves from the cold in their short winter, and to feed themselves with such meat as the soil affordeth: their meat is very well sodden, and they make broth very sweet and savoury. Their vessels are earthen pots, very large, white and sweet; their dishes are wooden platters of sweet timber. Within the place where they feed was their lodging, and within that their idol, which they worship, of whom they speak incredible things. While we were at meat, there came in at the gates two or three men with their bows and arrows from hunting, whom when we espied, we began to look one towards another, and offered to reach our weapons: but as soon as she espied our mistrust, she was very much moved, and caused some of her men to run out, and take away their bows and arrows and break them, and withal beat the poor fellows out of the gate again. When we departed in the evening and would not tarry all night, she was very sorry, and gave us into our boat our supper half-dressed, pots and all, and brought us to our boat

side, in which we lay all night, removing the same a
pretty distance from the shore. She perceiving our
jealousy, was much grieved, and sent divers men and
thirty women to sit all night on the bank side by us,
and sent us into our boats five mats to cover us from
the rain, using very many words to entreat us to rest
in their houses. But because we were few men, and
if we had miscarried the voyage had been in very
great danger, we durst not adventure anything, though
there was no cause of doubt; for a more kind and
loving people there cannot be found in the world, as
far as we have hitherto had trial.

Beyond this island there is the mainland, and over
against this island falleth into this spacious water
the great river called Occam by the inhabitants, on
which standeth a town called Pomeiock, and six days'
journey from the same is situate their greatest city,
called Skicoak, which this people affirm to be very
great: but the savages were never at it, only they
speak of it by the report of their fathers and other
men, whom they have heard affirm it to be above one
hour's journey about. Into this river falleth another
great river, called Cipo, in which there is found great
store of mussels, in which there are pearls; likewise
there descendeth into this Occam another river, called
Nomopana, on the one side whereof standeth a great
town called Chawanook, and the lord of that town
and country is called Pooneno. This Pooneno is not
subject to the king of Wingandacoa, but is a free lord.
Beyond this country is there another king, whom
they call Menatonon, and these three kings are in
league with each other. Towards the south-west,
four days' journey, is situate a town called Secotan,

which is the southermost town of Wingandacoa, near unto which, six-and-twenty years past there was a ship cast away, whereof some of the people were saved, and those were white people, whom the country people preserved. And after ten days remaining in an out island unhabited, called Wocokon, they with the help of some of the dwellers of Secotan, fastened two boats of the country together, and made masts unto them, and sails of their shirts, and having taken into them such victuals as the country yielded, they departed after they had remained in this out island three weeks. But shortly after, it seemed, they were cast away, for the boats were found upon the coast, cast a-land in another island adjoining. Other than these, there was never any people apparelled, or white of colour, either seen or heard of amongst these people, and these aforesaid were seen only of the inhabitants of Secotan; which appeared to be very true, for they wondered marvellously when we were amongst them at the whiteness of our skins, ever coveting to touch our breasts, and to view the same. Besides they had our ships in marvellous admiration, and all things else were so strange unto them, as it appeared that none of them had ever seen the like. When we discharged any piece, were it but an arquebus, they would tremble thereat for very fear, and for the strangeness of the same : for the weapons which themselves use are bows and arrows. The arrows are but of small canes, headed with a sharp shell or tooth of a fish sufficient enough to kill a naked man. Their swords be of wood hardened : likewise they use wooden breastplates for their defence. They have besides a kind of club, in the end whereof they fasten the sharp horns of a stag, or other beast.

Pomeiock. ("The town of Pomeiock, and true form of their houses, covered and enclosed, some with mats, and some with barks of trees, all compassed about with small poles stuck thick together instead of a wall")

When they go to wars they carry about with them their idol, of whom they ask counsel, as the Romans were wont of the oracle of Apollo. They sing songs as they march towards the battle, instead of drums and trumpets. Their wars are very cruel and bloody, by reason whereof, and of their civil dissensions which have happened of late years amongst them, the people are marvellously wasted, and in some places the country left desolate.

Adjoining to this country aforesaid, called Secotan, beginneth a country called Pomovik, belonging to another king, whom they call Piemacum; and this king is in league with the next king adjoining towards the setting of the sun, and the country Newsiok, situate upon a goodly river called Neus. These kings have mortal war with Wingina, king of Wingandacoa: but about two years past there was a peace made between the king Piemacum and the lord of Secotan, as these men which we have brought with us to England have given us to understand; but there remaineth a mortal malice in the Secotans, for many injuries and slaughters done upon them by this Piemacum. They invited divers men, and thirty women of the best of his country, to their town to a feast; and when they were altogether merry, and praying before their idol (which is nothing else but a mere illusion of the devil), the captain or lord of the town came suddenly upon them, and slew them every one, reserving the women and children; and these two have oftentimes since persuaded us to surprise Piemacum his town, having promised and assured us that there will be found in it great store of commodities. But whether their persuasion be to the end they may be revenged of their enemies, or for the love they bear to us, we leave that to the trial hereafter.

Beyond this island called Roanoak are many islands very plentiful of fruits and other natural increases, together with many towns and villages along the side of the continent, some bounding upon the islands, and some stretching up further into the land.

When we first had sight of this country, some thought the first land we saw to be the continent: but after we entered into the haven, we saw before us another mighty long sea, for there lieth along the coast a tract of islands two hundred miles in length, adjoining to the ocean sea, and between the islands two or three entrances. When you are entered between them (these islands being very narrow for the most part, as in most places six miles broad, in some places less, in few more) then there appeareth another great sea, containing in breadth in some places forty, and in some fifty, in some twenty miles over, before you come unto the continent: and in this enclosed sea there are above an hundred islands of divers bignesses, whereof one is sixteen miles long, at which we were, finding it a most pleasant and fertile ground, replenished with goodly cedars, and divers other sweet woods, full of currants, of flax, and many other notable commodities, which we at that time had no leisure to view. Besides this island there are many, as I have said, some of two, or three, of four, of five miles, some more, some less, most beautiful and pleasant to behold, replenished with deer, coneys, hares, and divers beasts, and about them the goodliest and best fish in the world, and in greatest abundance.

Thus, Sir, we have acquainted you with the particulars of our discovery made this present voyage, as far forth as the shortness of the time we there continued would afford us to take view of; and so contenting ourselves with this service at this time, which we hope hereafter to enlarge, as occasion and assistance shall be given, we resolved to leave the country, and to apply ourselves to return for England, which we did accordingly, and arrived safely in the west of England about the midst of September.

And whereas we have above certified you of the country taken in possession by us to her Majesty's use, and so to yours by her Majesty's grant, we thought good for the better assurance thereof to record some of the particular gentlemen, and men of account, who then were present, as witnesses of the same, that thereby all occasion of cavil to the title of the country, in her Majesty's behalf, may be prevented, which otherwise such as like not the action may use and pretend. Whose names are, Master Philip Amadas, Master Arthur Barlow, Captains; William Greenville, John Wood, James Bromewich, Henry Greene, Benjamin Wood, Simon Ferdinando, Nicholas Petman, John Hewes, of the company.

We brought home also two of the savages, being lusty men, whose names were Wanchese and Manteo.

NOTES

COLUMBUS: FIRST VOYAGE

I. A LETTER

The black figures refer to pages and the plain figures to lines

1, 15. Cadiz. Columbus started from Palos on August 3, 1492. Cadiz is a mistake for Gomera (one of the Canary Islands), whence he reached the West Indies in thirty-three days—September 8 to October 11. There were three vessels, the largest (in which Columbus himself sailed) was the *Santa Maria* of about 100 tons. The other two were caravels—decked fore and aft only—the *Pinta*, Captain Martin Alonso Pinzon, and the *Niña*, Captain Vicente Yañez Pinzon.

21. San Salvador. Watling Island.

24. Santa Maria de la Concepcion. Rum Cay.

2, 1. Fernandina. Long Island.

Isabella. Crooked Island.

Juana. Cuba. Columbus named it Juana in honour of Prince Juan, only son of Ferdinand and Isabella. He thought it was part of the mainland of China, and remained doubtful, even after the Indians had told him that it was an island.

7. Cathay. China.

4, 1. Española. Hispaniola, San Domingo, or Havti. He called it Española, because the country reminded him of Spain.

8, 15. blanca. A copper coin, worth about a quarter of a farthing.

11, 4. Navidad del Señor. The Nativity of our Lord. The flag-ship was wrecked here on Christmas Day.

6. as many men as I thought necessary. About forty, including one Englishman and one Irishman.

10. the King. Guacanagari.

33. Ethiopians. African natives.

12, 10, 11. **India**. Another version is apparently more correct: "except at an island which lies the second in one's way in coming to the Indies." Probably Dominica. Charis is probably for Carib, from which is derived the word "cannibal."

25. **Matenin**. Martinique.

13, 10. **navy**. A more correct version is "and slaves, as many of these idolaters as their Highnesses shall command to be shipped."

II. EXTRACTS FROM THE JOURNAL

15, 22. **Gran Can**. In 1260 Nicolo and Maffeo Polo left Constantinople, and reached the court of Kublai Khan, the Emperor of China. He sent them back as Ambassadors to the Pope, asking for missionaries to convert his people. They returned in 1269, and found that the Pope was dead, and no new one had been elected. The Polos, tired of.waiting for this election, started for the East again in 1271, together with their nephew Marco. The new Pope sent two Dominicans after them, but they lost heart and turned back.

16, 2. **Cristobal Colon**. The Spanish name for Columbus.

12. **January**. A misprint for March.

25. **three vessels**. See note p. 1, l. 15.

18, 31. **12 miles**. Columbus used Italian miles, four to a league.

19, 4. **land was first seen**. It was moonlight at 2 a.m. on Oct. 11.

33. **Guanahani**. See note p. 1, l. 21.

21, 6. **F and a Y**. Fernando and Ysabel.

24, 24. **blanca**. See note p. 8, l. 15.

32. **Cipango**. Japan. Marco Polo describes it in Book III, Ch. 2, as abounding in gold, pearls, and precious stones. When Columbus heard of Cuba, he thought it must be Cipango.

27, 8. **serpent**. Iguana.

28, 12. **Guisay**. Quinsay, or Kinsay (meaning "capital"). A flourishing sea-port in China, described by Marco Polo in Book II, Ch. 76.

29, 19. **there was any**. An obscure passage. Another version is: "and asked them if they had any there. They answered no, but made signs that there was plenty near, towards the S.E."

35, 11. **cazavi**. Cassava, prepared from the root of the manioc plant. Tapioca is purified cassava.

30. **Caribes**. See note p. 12, ll. 10, 11.

36, 5. **lombard**. A cannon.

COLUMBUS: SECOND VOYAGE

40, 4. **Gomera.** One of the Canary Islands.

17. **other vessels.** There were altogether seventeen, the flag-ship being the *Marigalante.*

41, 9. **the first.** Dominica, so named because it was discovered on a Sunday.

10. **the other.** Marigalante, after the ship in which Columbus sailed.

24. **the other island.** Marigalante.

42, 18. **very large island.** Guadaloupe.

44, 25. **this island.** Guadaloupe.

47, 21. **Ceyre.** Probably Dominica (the Charis or Carib of the First Voyage), the other two forming Guadaloupe.

49, 8. **another island.** Montserrat.

18. **another island appeared.** Santa Maria la Antigua.

51, 22. **an island.** St Martin.

23. **Ceyre.** Dominica. See note p. 47, l. 21.

51, 29. **point of land.** Santa Cruz.

52, 1. **forty islets.** Columbus named the largest St Ursula, and the rest The Eleven Thousand Virgins.

6. **lateen.** A lateen-sail is a triangular sail used in small boats, feluccas, etc., especially in the Mediterranean.

12. **Burenquen.** Puerto Rico (named by Columbus St John the Baptist).

53, 24. **another island.** Mona.

54, 31. **lizard.** An alligator.

56, 9. **Guacamari.** Guacanagari.

66, 7. **a port.** Port Dauphin.

67, 10. **an excellent harbour.** Port Isabella, thirty miles east of Monte Cristi.

22. **Marta.** Afterwards called Isabella.

68, 4. **ages.** Yams.

70, 26. **myrobalans.** Astringent plum-like fruit used in dyeing, tanning, etc.

71, 18. **to Spain.** He sent twelve ships, commanded by Antonio de Torres, to report what had happened (February, 1494). This letter of Dr Chanca's must have been brought by them. After the departure of de Torres, sickness broke out among the colonists, followed by a mutiny, which was quelled before the mutineers could seize the ships. Further reports of gold were brought, and

Columbus founded the Fort of St Thomas in the district of Cibao. Leaving a council to govern the two colonies, he again put to sea on April 24, 1494, to find if possible the coast of Cathay. During this voyage he discovered the island of Jamaica, and the cluster of little islands off the south coast of Cuba, which he called the Queen's Garden. He returned to Isabella at the end of September in a state of complete collapse, and was seriously ill for five months, tended by his brother Bartholomew, who had come from Spain with three ships laden with supplies. During the Admiral's absence the colonists treated the Indians with the utmost cruelty. Warfare ensued, and the Indians were crushed, and many taken as slaves, and a tribute was imposed upon the whole population of Española.

Meantime complaints about the despotic rule of Columbus had been carried back by disaffected colonists to Spain, and to answer these charges he left Isabella on March 10, 1496, and entered the Bay of Cadiz on June 11.

COLUMBUS: THIRD VOYAGE

74. 30. **terra firma.** He did not discover terra firma in the second voyage, but imagined the island of Cuba to be terra firma, because he was unable to explore it fully.

75, 26. **brazil-wood.** A hard red wood, yielding a dye. From it was derived the name of the country Brazil.

76, 13. **Sopora.** Ophir.

17. **Taprobana.** Ceylon.

77, 23. **the 30th of May.** In the year 1498.

78, 4. **an incorrect name.** They were named after Cape Verde, so-called owing to its green herbage, in contrast with Cape Blanco (the White Cape).

79, 29. **Cape Galea.** Now Cape Galeota, the most south-easterly point of the island of Trinidad.

82, 1. **Gracia.** Coast of Paria. Columbus did not know that he had discovered the mainland.

24. **upon the rocks.** Produced by the confluence of the Orinoco with the sea.

83, 12. **a channel.** Columbus named it the Serpent's Mouth, and the strait between Trinidad and the mainland at the north the Dragon's Mouth.

84, 5. **the Needle.** Now Point Alcatraz, or Point Pelican.

92, 12. **the "Adelantado."** Columbus had appointed his brother Bartholomew Lieutenant-Governor (Adelantado) of Española during his serious illness at Isabella in 1494.

22. **Thanks be to God.** This letter was sent from Española, where Columbus arrived at the end of August, 1498, after passing

and naming the island of Margarita on his way from Trinidad. He found the colony in confusion, as the colonists had broken into two parties, and two years passed before he could settle the dispute. Meantime complaints against the Admiral were being constantly carried to Ferdinand and Isabella. In consequence they sent Bobadilla to enquire into the condition of affairs in Española. He arrived in August, 1500, and acted in the most arbitrary manner, put Columbus and his brothers in chains, and sent them back to Spain. The monarchs repudiated Bobadilla's action, and promised Columbus compensation. Nevertheless they appointed Ovando as governor in his place.

CARTIER: SECOND VOYAGE

98, 8. two wild men. In the previous voyage they had carried off two natives to France, and now had these men on board.

12. Canada. Then applied to the country about Quebec.

14. Saguenay. Now part of the Province of Quebec. The River Saguenay is a tributary of the St Lawrence.

23. Island of the Assumption. Anticosti, the island at the entrance of the River St Lawrence. Cartier, ignorant of the strait between Newfoundland and Nova Scotia, had coasted part of Newfoundland, and sailed through the Strait of Belle Isle.

99, 7. river of Hochelaga. The River St Lawrence. Hochelaga is now Montreal.

19. any passage might be discovered. He hoped to find a northern strait into the Pacific, as Magellan had done in the South.

31. Round Islands. Seven Islands, to the north-west of Anticosti.

100, 10. a river. River Saguenay.

102, 25. Island of Filberts. Isle aux Coudres.

30. ten leagues in length. Isle of Orleans.

103, 12. millet. Maize.

104, 23. a little river. St Charles River.

105, 10. Stadacona. Quebec.

106, 3. Bacchus Island. See note p. 102, l. 30.

23. Hochelaga. Montreal.

114, 31. turtles. Turtle-doves.

115, 1. great wide lake. Lake St Peter.

116, 2. a coney. A rabbit.

119, 3. Bresil. Brazil.

8. Mount Royal. Which has given its name to Montreal.

129, 32. Bresil. See note p. 119, l. 3.

131, 22. sea-horses. Walruses.

135, 15. cruel disease. Scurvy.

138, 21. passing. More than.

144, 20. Franciscus, etc. Francis the First reigns, by the grace of God King of the French.

149, 18. Island of Hares. Still called Hare Island.

29. Port of Chaleur. Chaleur Bay, between the Province of Quebec and New Brunswick. Cartier discovered it during his previous voyage, in July, 1534, and owing to the warmth of the place, gave it this name.

151, 12. Cape Race. The south-east point of Newfoundland, named after the Pointe du Raz in Brittany. They had sailed back through the Strait of Belle Isle, and down the east coast of the island.

GILBERT'S VOYAGE

153, 10. Edward Hayes. Captain and owner of the *Golden Hind*.

17. Cawset Bay. Cawsand Bay, near Plymouth.

22. Admiral. The ship in which the commander of a fleet sailed. He was called the General.

154, 17. hobby-horse. A wicker horse used in morris-dances.

155, 15. Newfoundland. This name then included the modern Newfoundland and the neighbouring lands, such as Nova Scotia.

21. traverse. A zigzag line.

157, 17. Baccalaos. "The country of cod fish." The name was given to the north-west part of the newly-discovered lands.

18. Cape St Francis. In the south-east of the island of Newfoundland, near St John's.

159, 20. fights. Canvas, or bulk-heads, set up before a sea-fight to conceal the men.

28. butt. A bow-shot.

31. sea-gate. Current.

161, 5. rusk. Ship's biscuit.

29. raspis berries. Raspberries.

163, 8. fee farm. Land held by the tenant and his heirs at a yearly rent.

164, 5. cards. Charts.

165, 31. raspises. See note p. 161, l. 29.

166, 13. **letted.** Hindered.

168, 11. **near expired.** The patent, granted in June, 1578, was to expire in six years.

17. **bruit.** Report.

169, 28. **fights.** See note p. 159, l. 20.

170, 25. **Sablon.** Sable Island, off Nova Scotia. The 60th degree of longitude, and the 44th of latitude both pass through it.

172, 13. **harping iron.** Harpoon.

173, 17. **sea room.** Clear space for allowing a ship to turn, etc.

"Give us but a good ship and sea room, and we think nothing of such a squall of wind as that."

Robinson Crusoe (Golden Treasury edition, p. 7).

22. **cock.** Cockboat (small ship's boat).

174, 3. **Hungarian.** A scholar, Stephen Parmenius, whom Gilbert had taken with him.

6. **gests.** Deeds.

15. **overseen.** Deceived.

180, 10. **a northern man altogether.** There were two rival schools of opinion with regard to the colonization of America. One held that a beginning should be made in the south (in Florida, to the north-east of the Gulf of Mexico): the other, that the fishing-grounds of Newfoundland should be the starting-point.

181, 16. **over hard.** Over hardy, rash.

AMADAS AND BARLOW'S VOYAGE

184, 4. **Virginia.** So named by Queen Elizabeth. This is now part of North Carolina, the modern Virginia being further north.

5. **one of the said captains.** Arthur Barlow.

16. **diurnal.** Now "journal." Daily record, or log-book.

185, 8. **disboguing.** Disemboguing (pouring forth at the mouth, or discharging).

31. **arquebus.** An early kind of portable gun, supported on a rest, or by a hook on a tripod.

187, 21. **mean.** Middle, or moderate.

23. **any of both ways.** Either way.

191, 20. **buff.** Buffalo.

194, 8. **in gage.** As a pledge.

196, 8. **Roanoak.** Now Roanoke, in North Carolina between Albemarle Sound and Pamlico Sound. A colony was founded here next year (1585).   There is also a river Roanoke, which flows into Albemarle Sound.

13.   **artificially.**   Skilfully.

22.   **utter.**   Outer.

199, 3.   **jealousy.**   Suspiciousness.

27.   **Chawanook.**   The district of Chawanook was between Albemarle Sound and Chesapeake Bay.

200, 6.   **Wocokon.**   Ocracoke, at the entrance of Pamlico Sound.

www.ingramcontent.com/pod-product-compliance
Ingram Content Group UK Ltd.
Pitfield, Milton Keynes, MK11 3LW, UK
UKHW042142280225
455719UK00001B/51